CONCORDIA UNIVERSITY
DD67.F65
GERMAN AFTER WAR PROBLEM
S0-GGI-742
3 4211 000022959

GERMAN AFTER-WAR PROBLEMS

LONDON : HUMPHREY MILFORD
OXFORD UNIVERSITY PRESS

GERMAN AFTER-WAR PROBLEMS

BY

KUNO FRANCKE

CAMBRIDGE
HARVARD UNIVERSITY PRESS
1927

COPYRIGHT, 1927
BY THE PRESIDENT AND FELLOWS OF
HARVARD COLLEGE

Second impression

PRINTED AT THE HARVARD UNIVERSITY PRESS
CAMBRIDGE, MASS., U. S. A.

FOREWORD

THE papers here collected reflect observations made during various visits to my native country in the years following the Treaty of Versailles: in 1920, when the effects of war and starvation were still visible everywhere; in 1923, when the Ruhr invasion and the inflation disaster seemed to be heading the country into chaos; in 1926, the year of Germany's entry into the League of Nations. These dates in themselves speak of the extraordinary recuperative power shown by the German people during these six years of poverty and distress. What some of the intellectual and moral forces were which made this remarkable advance toward national recovery and international coöperation possible, I have tried briefly to set forth in this little book.

The first three essays are here reprinted from *The Atlantic Monthly*.

K. F.

November, 1926

CONTENTS

I
INTELLECTUAL CURRENTS IN CONTEMPORARY GERMANY (1924) 3

II
A GERMAN VOICE OF HOPE (1925) 35

III
GERMAN CHARACTER AND THE GERMAN-AMERICAN (1926) 68

IV
GERMAN AFTER-WAR IMAGINATION (1926) . 95

INDEX 129

GERMAN AFTER-WAR PROBLEMS

I

INTELLECTUAL CURRENTS IN CONTEMPORARY GERMANY
(1924)

THE intellectual life of the Germany of to-day may be summed up by a word of Nietzsche's: "The Germans have as yet no to-day; they are of the day before yesterday and of the day after to-morrow." For perhaps never has the tragic truth of this word been more impressively revealed than now.

It is indeed hard to see how the German of to-day can obtain a view of the present in any way satisfying or acceptable. Wherever he looks, he sees popular misery, foreign oppression, national disintegration and decay. How, then, could it be otherwise but that the whole trend of contemporary German thought should turn either toward the shades of the past or the yet unborn forms of the future?

GERMAN AFTER-WAR PROBLEMS

I

Memories of the past are naturally uppermost in the minds of the older generation, especially that part of it which preëminently shared in the splendor of the Wilhelminian age: the bureaucracy, the army and navy, the university professors, the landed and industrial aristocracy. How everything seemed to flourish and progress in the powerful Empire founded by the Iron Chancellor! German industry and commerce encircled the globe. German city administration was recognized all over the world as an unequaled model of civic efficiency and integrity. The social legislation of the Empire assured to the German working class a material basis of living such as no other country offered. The universal military service guaranteed a bodily vigor of the broad masses and a widely diffused sense of public duty, perhaps more sharply pronounced than anywhere else. The German universities and polytechnics were unquestionably the most productive institutions of research in the world and attracted a body of students who in methodical training and thoroughness of scholarship surpassed the youth of most other countries. The cultivation of art, particularly of music and the stage, was valued in a much higher degree than elsewhere as a public task, and had led in the widest circles of the population to a susceptibility to artistic impressions and to an intensity of interest in æsthetic questions which again had hardly a parallel among other peoples.

That this mighty empire and this brilliant civilization rested after all upon feet of clay, that they had been put in the service of a policy which ignored the fundamental conditions of healthy progress, respect for personal freedom and earnest desire for international brotherhood, and therefore was bound to conjure up fatal conflicts within and without — this is a truth which was hardly realized even by the most enlightened before the war. That its realization to-day should come particularly hard to those who themselves were instruments of that policy — the intellectuals of the old régime — is easy to understand. And yet, what a service could these intellectuals have rendered to the young struggling German Republic, and thereby to the Fatherland, if they, particularly the teachers in the Gymnasia and the university professors, had whole-heartedly accepted the new political responsibilities which the collapse of the old order brought for them; if they had earnestly pledged themselves to the Weimar Constitution and the ideals of popular government contained in it; if they had made themselves the mouthpiece of an enlightened internationalism. Instead of that, a defiant pessimism seems to have settled upon the minds of most of these men. They take no part in the efforts to substitute a new public consciousness for the played-out monarchy; they ascribe all popular misery to what they call Socialist misrule or Jewish conspiracy; they rail at all measures of internal reform; they clamor for a return to Bismarckian principles; they even acclaim the methods of a Ludendorff.

This atmosphere of resentment and despair is reflected in a book which as no other work of scholarship has fascinated German readers of the last half decade: Oswald Spengler's "Doom of the Occident" (*Der Untergang des Abendlandes*). That this book [1] is in its way an extraordinary achievement cannot be gainsaid. It is a brilliant specu-

---

[1] Although conceived before the War and largely written during it, its message is essentially an appeal to the after-war state of mind. An English translation under the title *The Decline of the West* appeared in 1926 (Knopf, New York).

INTELLECTUAL CURRENTS

lative survey of the higher life of the European nations, including their Oriental predecessors and winding up with the present. It is saturated with learning, it presents a vast amount of organized material, it abounds in striking characterizations both of individual figures and of general movements. Its most original contribution to the philosophy of history is, however, the pervading thought of a contrast between culture and civilization.

The customary division of European history into ancient, mediæval, and modern times Spengler replaces by the conception of a multitude of individual, autochthonous cultures, each of which has its own "soul"; and the customary assumption of a continuity of development from one national culture to another he replaces by the thesis that each individual culture completes its own circle of life separately, from infancy to manhood, senility, and utter extinction. The senile age of culture is civilization; in other words, civilization is that stage of human development when the soul-life of a given culture has become torpid, when unconscious production has been hardened into conscious reflection, when the dynamic has given way to the mechanic, when science takes the place of art, when the chief concern is no longer the creation of ideas, but only their diffusion among the largest possible number of people.

The rise and decay of three indigenous cultures Spengler singles out for particular study, the life-span of each of which he estimates at about a thousand years: Græco-Roman culture, ending with the Augustan age; Arab culture, having its roots in the same soil that brought forth Christianity, and withering away about the eleventh century; Occidental culture, rising in the eleventh century and now nearing its doom. The "soul" of Græco-Roman culture he designates as Apollinic; the "soul" of Arab culture as magic; the "soul" of Occidental culture as Faust-like. With special emphasis he contrasts the first and the last of these types with each other. The Apollinic soul consists in calm and clarity, the Faust-like soul in unrest and longing. Græco-Roman culture consequently finds its highest expression in the mastery of the finite, Occidental culture in the striving for the infinite. The genius of the former is plastic, the genius of the latter musical. The universe of the former is Ptolemaic, the universe of the latter Copernican. The one produces Euclidean geometry, the other the differential calculus of Leibniz. The one leads to the Aristotelian philosophy of the actual, the other to Kantian Transcendentalism. In short, in every sphere of life a fundamental contrast between classical and modern culture.

But this very polarity of their psychic character brings out all the more clearly the parallelism in the external development of these two — as indeed of all — individual cultures in rise and decay. With Alexander the Great, Greek culture entered upon its senility; it turned into civilization; it no longer produced new ideas, but only put the old ideas into wider circulation. The senile age of Occidental culture set in at the beginning of the nineteenth century, with Napoleonic imperialism. The Faust-like soul of the Occident has lived itself out. It has realized all its possibilities. It has exhausted itself in philosophy and religion, in art and science. The only work left is collecting and classifying what has been achieved and applying it to practical purposes. Not the creation of new ideals of culture, but a life in the service of civilization is the demand of the hour. And the only hope of the future lies in a new Cæsar or a generation of Cæsars able to weld all the forces of civilization into one mighty mechanism which will keep automatically in motion until it wears out.

"If under the impression of this book" — these are Spengler's own words — "youths of the new generation should turn to the hammer instead of the pen, to the rudder instead of the brush, to politics instead of metaphysics, they would do what I wish, and I could not wish anything better for them." Without sentimental wailings, to prepare ourselves for the coming doom is the only becoming thing. "The ancient world died without foreboding its death. We know our history. We shall die with full consciousness; we shall follow all the stages of our own dissolution with the keen eye of the experienced physician."

No wonder that the brilliant paradoxes and daring affirmations of Spengler, in a time dark with despair, were welcomed and feverishly consumed as a sort of soporific. But it certainly cannot be said that this self-constituted physician of his age has contributed much to its health. What the world — and especially Germany — needs today is a new faith, a new hope of the future. All the intellectual and moral forces of the people should be summoned to the service of inner regeneration. The conviction should be planted in all hearts that from the ruin of the old Germany a new and better Germany must arise. Spengler does everything he can to stifle this conviction. Rooted solely in the past, he has lost the sense for the meaning of the present, and the future is a blank to him. He, the admirer of Greek tragedy, the keen student of Shakespeare, the reveler in Bach and Beethoven, the disciple of Goethe and Nietzsche, demands from his contemporaries that they renounce all higher aspirations and strivings and chain themselves, in fatalistic contempt of the world, to the practical routine of the day. Why? Because he thinks the age doomed to perdition; because he believes that the death knell of Occidental culture has struck. For the sake of this whim, like a modern Cato, he calls upon his fellow countrymen to commit moral suicide.

II

Fortunately, a more productive form of relief from the distressing present than this exclusive dwelling in the past is afforded by the innate German love of work and the innate German interest in the affairs of the spirit, which have stood the test even of the desperate material conditions of to-day. The mental concentration which enabled

Spengler to bring to its consummation, in the midst of national disaster, a work of such massive learning and such marked originality is itself a striking illustration of this fact. But it is not an isolated illustration.

Nothing perhaps is a greater surprise to the American traveling in Germany to-day than the undiminished scientific and artistic zeal making itself felt everywhere. Large museum buildings, such as the Pergamon Museum and the German Museum at Berlin, are, in spite of all difficulties, being slowly carried forward toward completion. Last autumn the city of Augsburg devoted a whole week to the study of Romanticism, through addresses of prominent scholars on Romantic literature, exhibitions of Romantic painting, and performances of the works of Romantic composers and dramatists. This winter, even the smaller German cities offer a regular repertoire of drama and opera far exceeding in seriousness and dignity theatrical conditions in Boston or Chicago. And professors of many different German universities were unanimous in telling me last summer that they never had had such students as now. A feverish thirst for learning, they said, seemed to have taken possession of them; and no privations or

INTELLECTUAL CURRENTS

hardships, no unheated rooms, no lack of light, no empty stomachs, no threadbare clothes, no difficulties in obtaining a book or scientific instrument, no hard bodily work in factories or warehouses could dampen the enthusiasm with which these youths plunged into intellectual pursuits. It was natural that under pressure of economic distress a majority of the students should turn to the technical and exact sciences; but the humanistic studies also, such as philosophy, history of literature, history of art, showed no marked decrease in numbers and surpassed former times by the ardor and devotion of their followers.

These testimonies of professors are borne out by many manifestations of university life that have come to my notice: artistic achievements such as the annual Händel festivals at Göttingen; welfare movements such as the widespread activity of student organizations in support of Professor Damaschke's schemes of land-holding reform; moral efforts such as the propaganda of the Eucken Alliance for cultivation of liberal and enlightened religious views — all symptoms of an academic idealism which in the midst of national collapse stands out for the reconstruction and heightening of individual life.

GERMAN AFTER-WAR PROBLEMS

It was my good fortune, twice during the last few years, to take part in an academic celebration which revealed in a most impressive manner this spirit of unquenchable idealism: the so-called *Kieler Herbstwoche für Kunst und Wissenschaft* (Kiel Autumnal Week for Art and Science). Well known is the old Kieler Woche, an international regatta instituted by the former Emperor as a German counterpart to the famous "Cowes Week." Twelve years ago, I was present at this old Kieler Woche, and I shall never forget the fine June day when from the Imperial yacht Hohenzollern I saw the beautiful Kiel harbor before me filled with the vessels of all nations, a large part of the German navy arrayed in gala formation, the flags flying from all steeples and houses of the town, and a festive multitude crowding the shores and the streets. Then came the war and the collapse. But in the autumn of 1920 I could witness the first new Kieler Woche — not an imperial naval review and sporting event, but a feast of science and art, arranged by the University and the City of Kiel, and supported by eminent scholars and artists from all over Germany. In the deserted harbor there lay the last sad remnants of what had once been the proud German navy; the last great German floating dock was being put in readiness for the tugs that were to tow it away to England; from the distance there were heard the dull reports of the blasting of the surrounding forts. But all this did not seem to affect the people of Kiel. Again the city had put on its array of flags; again a festive crowd moved through the streets; and young and old, high and low seemed bent only upon showing what this new Kieler Woche was to be: a holiday of the spirit.

The festivities began on Saturday evening with a private performance, by members of the University, of Goethe's little allegorical play, *Palæophron and Neoterpe* — the old time and the new conversing with each other and forming a covenant for the future. On Sunday morning there were special services in all the churches, in the afternoon a performance of Beethoven's *Missa Solemnis*, in the evening Hauptmann's *Weavers*. And then followed six days of such a wealth of intellectual and spiritual treats as it is hard to describe. Every forenoon an address by some leading man from the foremost of German universities, beginning with Einstein on the theory of relativity and ending with the Rector of Bonn University on the comparative study of law. Every afternoon some symphony or oratorio. And every evening both a drama and an opera of the highest rank, the dramas leading from Goethe's *Egmont* to Byron's *Manfred*, the operas culminating in Wagner's *Meistersinger*. Never have I seen an audience stirred to such a height of feeling as at this performance of the *Meistersinger*. It seemed as if Hans Sachs, represented by Feinhals of Munich with perfect art, was instinctively felt to be the embodiment of the very best in German character, its simplicity, purity, earnestness, its proud modesty, and its moral strength. He was joyously acclaimed as the genius of his people, as a pledge of the national future. One forgot the stage; one forgot the anguish of the present; one seemed to see a time when Germany, drawing forth new life from the deepest roots of her being, will again take her place, admired and beloved, among the nations.

Last autumn I had again the privilege of sharing in this University Week of my native town. One hardly sees how it was possible to plan such a celebration under the present chaotic conditions of German life, and one cannot admire enough the courage which inspired the organizers to the following announcement of their programme:

INTELLECTUAL CURRENTS

"Joy has become a rare guest amongst us; economic and political disasters threaten to crush us. And yet we have dared, this year also, in simple forms befitting the time, to arrange an autumnal week for Art and Science. For more than ever do we need an opportunity to lift ourselves, through earnest introspection and noble enjoyment, above the cares of the day."

This time there were no flags from the housetops, there was no festive crowd in the streets. But again a number of other German universities had sent their representatives, again actors and singers from the foremost German theatres took part, and again a programme of genuine worth was carried through. The academic addresses related for the most part to the age of the Renaissance and the Reformation. The musical part was in the main a memorial tribute to Max Reger: his widow had been invited as a guest of honor, and almost every day brought a performance, mostly in churches, of one of his great compositions. The dramatic series began with *King Lear* and led through Strindberg's *Spectre-Sonata* and a dramatization of Holbein's *Dance of Death* to Hugo von Hofmannsthal's *Everyman*. In short, this time also the Kieler Herbstwoche contained enough of beauty and thought to raise both contributors and recipients to a higher level and to impart to them strength for the inevitable sufferings of cruel reality.

"We need such a store of food for the coming winter" was one of the touching words of thanks which I heard after an address which I myself had been invited to deliver during this week.

III

All the academic efforts thus far considered are after all only makeshifts or diversions. They contain nothing essentially new; they derive strength from the ideals and achievements of former generations. But there is no lack of efforts in contemporary Germany which at least make the claim of offering something essentially new and of pointing the way from the misery of the present to a freer and nobler conception of humanity.

Three remarkable men who, each in his own way, stand for this new ideal of life I shall attempt briefly to characterize: Friedrich Wilhelm Foerster, Rudolf Steiner, and Count Hermann Keyserling.

Foerster is a much-disputed figure. To some he is anathema, a traitor to his country; by others he is acclaimed as a leader and as a prophet of true national greatness. Perhaps he has gone too far in his condemnation of German policy of the last decades — at least during the war it would have been wiser not to seem to abet the defamation of Germany by her enemies. But a genuine patriot Foerster is, nevertheless, and the martyrdom of conviction surrounds him with the halo of tragic experience.

For him, the salvation of Germany lies in the radical turning away from the Bismarckian policy of centralization and the appeal to might. Germany, he thinks, by her national temper as well as by her geographical position, is predestined to become the great mediator in European life. Federalism, in his opinion, was always the fundamental principle of German internal politics; and in foreign affairs the tolerant and cosmopolitan German was naturally averse both to the narrow, centralized nationalism of the French, and to the harsh imperialism of the English. The imitation of these altogether un-German tendencies by the Prussian monarchy had been the ruin of the German State. In the first place externally. For by the appeal to might, a people living in the midst of neighboring rivals was bound to condemn itself to being overpowered by them; in its own interest it should have appealed to reason instead of to might. But spiritually also Bismarckian policy had damaged and impoverished the German people by forcing the wealth of its tribal individualities into the rigid pattern of militarism.

From these aberrations the German soul must be freed. The individual German must become again what he was in the classic age of German culture: a citizen of the world. And German policy must find its highest task in helping to lay the foundation of a true League of Nations.

"In order to save ourselves from becoming the centre of war between East and West, we must become the centre of peace. In view of the tremendous tension of the present world situation, the aim of the new German policy must be everywhere to unite and adjust instead of splitting up and intriguing. We must, with tact and loyalty, see to it that the German question is not going to sow discord between the other Governments. In every dissension we must honestly work for European unity and for world accord. On every occasion — even in questions that do not affect us immediately — we must try to smooth out the difficulties of our former enemies, and in every individual case we must help all parties to arrive at a morally fruitful compromise. A German foreign policy of this sort would at once be recognized as a blessing to the world. Through it we should atone for the dynamite policy of the former, militaristic Germany; we should open new paths to all other nations. Thus the one forcibly disarmed people might save the rest of the world from its own armaments."

In the face of the policy of conquest and oppression which militaristic France is at present pursuing on the Rhine and Ruhr, such words as these will appear to many as the childlike fancies of a day-dreamer. And yet, do they not spring from motives which ought to become general — motives which, if made general, would indeed usher in a new and better era of humanity? And would the vanquished and mutilated Germany not achieve a moral victory more glorious than her military defeat was crushing, if she indeed succeeded by such a policy of reconciliation in kindling that same spirit in her former enemies? A liberating force these thoughts are, in any case. They free from the dull pressure of suffering by making us see the meaning of suffering. They turn our glance toward ideals, the mere pursuit of

GERMAN AFTER-WAR PROBLEMS

which, irrespective of success or failure, sets all the highest instincts of our being in motion.

Rudolf Steiner also — the originator of the German variety of contemporary theosophical thought — aims at the creation of a new consciousness of international solidarity. It is significant that he should call his system of ideas, not theosophy but anthroposophy — science of man, not of God. He shares with the Indo-English-American theosophists the belief in the spirituality of the universe and the striving for an ever-heightened spiritualization of the individual. But he is distinguished from them by holding aloof from all manner of occultism and by the absorption of the whole tradition of German intellectual history. The name "Goetheanum," borne by the central sanctuary of the widely spread communities of his followers, is a visible symbol of his intellectual breadth. And much more energetically than any of his spiritual brethren of other nationalities he devotes himself to the problems of social reform.

Here again it is symptomatic of the course which a considerable current of contemporary German thought is taking, that Steiner also sees the deepest cause of the German collapse in the overstraining of the national conception of the State. The German State, according to him, had encroached arbitrarily upon the other two principal spheres of public activity, the industrial and the cultural. The urgent need of to-day, therefore, is to make the three fundamental forms of social life — State, industry, and culture — independent of each other, and to recognize each of these forms in its individuality and special task. The State, Steiner thinks, has to do only with the legal relation of man to man, or, as Super-State, with the legal relation of people to people. If it tries, itself, to carry on industrial enterprises, if it tries to regulate intellectual production, then it loses thereby the power to fulfill its own mission, the nonpartisan administration of justice; it becomes party itself; nay, it becomes the tyrant of society.

This was indeed, according to Steiner, the condition of Germany before the war. Brilliant as was the development of German industry during the last fifty years, industry, through its close connection with the State, had become an instrument of politics and had thereby called forth political frictions all over the world. And even the much-admired social legislation of the Empire, the invalid and old-age insurance, had been robbed of its inner worth by the fact that it was planned as a political measure for the curbing of Social Democracy and therefore failed to win over the hearts of the laboring class.

Steiner takes a similar view of the scientific and artistic production and the whole educational system of the old Empire. Schools, universities, and academies of art were, in his opinion, only too often managed as breeding-places of a particular set of political views, and, in so far as this was the case, were made to serve purposes alien to their real task. In spite of their undoubted technical efficiency and in spite of many individual achievements of research made possible by them, they accordingly — as a whole — fell short of the chief goal of all education: the creation of a free, broad, unbiased, universally human conception of life. In a word, great as were the successes achieved by the German Empire during the last fifty years, by concentrating the energy of a whole people upon the immediately attainable and the nationally useful, this Empire has not fulfilled a far-reaching and lasting international mission.

It is for the defeated and humiliated Germany to fulfill such a mission, by emancipating the

INTELLECTUAL CURRENTS

three fundamental forms of social life from each other. A State which limits its activity to safeguarding equal rights for all, which does not aspire to being an industrial overlord or an intellectual dictator, is certain in its relation with other countries likewise to avoid encroachment upon legitimate rights. An industrial system which does not serve political interests is certain to carry on its intercourse with foreign industrial systems in the spirit of international compromise, not of international threats. An intellectual life which is permitted to develop without any political interference, spontaneously and from within, is certain to seek out its kindred in other countries also and, by amalgamating with them, to help in producing a truly international mind and a living consciousness of the unity of the human race.

Here lie the most portentous, and the most hopeful, tasks of the German future.

Count Keyserling is the most brilliant of the three men considered here in common. The spirited observer of life who in happier days traveled around the globe in order to find himself, who, after the return to his ancestral estate in Esthonia, was plunged through the war into the conflict between his German blood and allegiance to a hostile Government, and finally, through the Russian revolution, was bereft of everything and sent into exile, has now for years placed himself resolutely and without reserve in the service of European reconstruction; and from his "School of Wisdom" in Darmstadt, from before the very gates of foreign oppression and misrule, there come forth ever new words of life and inspiration.

Keyserling is not, like Foerster, an unconditional pacifist; the repulse of attacks upon the foundations of national existence is for him a matter of course. Nor is he, like Foerster and Steiner, an absolute opponent of the Bismarckian conception of the State. But the past is for him something irrevocably dead; he condemns any attempt to restore its forms; he lives altogether in the future; in the present he sees only and wants to see only the new emerging from the ruins of the old.

He says:

"Perhaps never before was a people, as a thing of the past, so entirely done for as the German people to-day. The heroic figures of its great tradition are gone; the representatives of its most

INTELLECTUAL CURRENTS

recent past have proved incapable of satisfying the demands of a new spirit of the times. Neither the Prussian officer, nor the official, nor the professor, nor even the technical expert, as traditional types, can be depended upon as leaders in the work of reconstruction. But on the other hand, never before did a people in like circumstances bear so much future in itself. It is the most youthful, most virile, most promising people of all Europe. Thanks to the breadth of its intellectual basis and to the afflux of fresh elements through the immigration of exiled Germans from abroad, it has suffered less in quality through the war than most other belligerents.

"Now its task is to understand its character and its mission correctly and to remodel its type accordingly. Since types are creations of the spirit, such a remodeling is always possible; and Germans are particularly easy to remodel, since no other people is so easily influenced by ideas. If Germany remodels herself in accordance with the needs of the time, then her speedy rise is beyond all question. For she has before her a goal of such tremendous import that all the experiences of the past pale before it."

What is this goal? Keyserling has tried to answer this question chiefly from two points of view, the political and the industrial.

The assurance of a great political task of Germany for the new Europe Keyserling finds, paradoxically, in the essentially unpolitical character of the German people. Politics, in the diplomatic sense of the word, as a manifestation of the national craving for power, is doomed — he thinks — to play in the future only a secondary rôle.

Inadequate as have been, hitherto, the attempts to regulate the relations of countries with each other through the resort to an international court, the whole development of modern civilization nevertheless inevitably leads to the conception of humanity as a unit, within which the claims of individual nations for power must be subordinated to the law of the whole. The rule of might is therefore bound more and more to lose caste, to appear as something second-rate, something out of date.

Now the German character is conspicuously unfit for wielding might; and it was a fatal mistake of the Wilhelminian age not to have taken account of this national peculiarity. In spite of Nietzsche's hysterical cries for power and mastery, the German character stands, essentially, not for power and mastery but for insight and understanding. The average German likes to adapt himself rather than to rule; he is less organizing than organizable; his patriotism — in so far as it is not simply feeling for home — rests not so much on pride in political dominion as on appreciation of æsthetic and spiritual creations. The chief motives of his moral conduct are truthfulness, conscientiousness, objectivity, respect for higher values, diligence, joy of work — in other words, the less the German is fitted to be a politician, the more valuable is he as a citizen.

The political service of the German people for Europe should therefore consist in demonstrating the superiority of citizenship over politics, by creating a model democracy and a model socialistic State. The old State has paved the way for such a change in many directions. What is needed now is to instill a new spirit, the spirit of freedom, into the old organization; to break entirely away from the principle of class; to appraise the workman, not as a marketable commodity, but as a member of society; and thus, not so much to fulfill the Socialistic party programme as to carry out the fundamental principle of Socialism: that every man must be treated, not only as a means to an end, but above all as an end in himself.

"This task of supreme importance could and should be accomplished by Germany, the only land of the Occident where knowledge predominates over the will, where everyone has his own individual view of the world and guides his own activity thereby. If, however, Germany does accomplish this task, then she is sure of an immense proselyting power. For everywhere in the Occidental world there exists the same longing for this new life; and it is only a question of where first it will come to fulfillment."

An equally wide horizon Count Keyserling opens up to the German people in industrial life. Not only the policy of might is — as we have heard — destined to play a comparatively subordinate part in international affairs of the future: the State itself is bound to lose more and more in importance as compared with the great industrial combinations.

"Even before the war the internal balance of power had shifted in this direction. The greatness of England rested to no small degree in the fact that she had fallen behind politically, in so far as the idea of Empire was borne, besides the

INTELLECTUAL CURRENTS

State, by a variety of other free organizations. America's marvelous rise resulted largely from the circumstance that there the State left leadership in industrial development to the enterprise of private corporations. As to Germany, her true power among the nations — which was far greater than most Germans knew — did not rest so much upon her army, which after all was only continental, as upon the fine meshes of her industrial cobweb, spanning the globe; and this power was destroyed only because the German Government carried on a policy inimical to the true interests of German industry, so that the true power of the country was overruled by the spirit of what in reality was the most insignificant and impotent part of the national body."

To-day the defeated, feeble, bankrupt German State is not in a position to take part in national reconstruction in any other way beyond what has already been indicated — the suffusion of public life with democratic and socialistic ideals. The actual task of reconstruction lies with the leaders of industry, the heads of the great private corporations. The Syndicate of the "Associated German Industries" means more than Government and Reichstag put together. Now the interests of these industrial combinations themselves demand supra-national agreement. For them, more than for any other group of society, it is a question of the reconstruction — not of any single people, but of Europe. In their own interest, therefore, they must work for international reconciliation, for a real peace.

The great question of to-day is, Will the German industrial leaders be equal to their task? Will they be conscious of the fact that they are not private individuals, but rulers responsible to the national conscience and responsible for the national welfare? Will they refuse in common with the invaders of the Ruhr to enslave German workingmen and to sell German sovereignty of German soil? Will they see that the moment has come for them to demonstrate by great acts their right to assume the leadership formerly left to the State? In other words, will they save the German national dignity and the German soil? Will they actually carry out the socialization of the State, demanded by the age? Will they, by genuine international fraternization, permanently secure the peace of Europe?

Should the industrial leaders fail to live up to this momentous task, should they for personal

INTELLECTUAL CURRENTS

gain sacrifice national sovereignty and the vital interests of the German workmen, then Germany's last hour has come, then Bolshevism will destroy the last vestiges of German greatness of the past. But if the leaders of industry grasp the momentousness of their task and show themselves equal to it, then a new era of German achievements in industrial life also is assured. For it was her industrial organization which gave Germany her leadership before the war. If this organization now fills itself with the new spirit of democracy and of international accord, if thereby it comes to be the embodiment of the collective work of the whole people and the foremost representative of European unity, then Germany will be able— not, as heretofore, isolated, but in conjunction with the rest of the world— to employ her best strength.

"Not only the Prussian but also the nationalistic period of German history belongs irrevocably to the past. But it means more and is more fruitful to be a foremost part of progressive humanity than to maintain one's self against all other nations. It means more to work for the benefit of all than for one's self alone. In the new, industrially united world the best qualities of the German mind will soon assert themselves and will bring back to Germany the human leadership which, in other forms, she had in the classic epoch of our literature and philosophy."

Men like Foerster, Steiner, and Keyserling are perhaps too prone to overlook the obstacles which block the way to the goal seen afar from the height of their intuitive hopes. Surely, only the purest faith and the most exalted self-renunciation will be able to pass unscathed through the ordeals which beset the path of the German future from all sides. But even though the immediate future is dark, it means much to have men of this stamp point to the distant peaks on the horizon. The growth of a new national type which will unite the best traditions of the past with the stern exigencies of the present, seems in the long run assured.

II

A GERMAN VOICE OF HOPE
(1925)

I

COUNT HERMANN KEYSERLING has recently attracted international attention through brilliant and intensely original essays on political and industrial subjects of the day. It would, however, be a mistake to think of him chiefly as a man interested in contemporary problems of practical affairs. What he really stands for is a moral reconstruction of Europe, a fundamental and abiding remodeling of the spiritual structure of the individual, a new outlook upon life in all its higher possibilities. An analysis of this inspiring personality from a somewhat wider point of view seems worth while.

Keyserling belongs to that Baltic nobility of German stock which for centuries has been one of the foremost outposts of German culture on Slavic soil. The history of his family contains a goodly number of names prominent in the annals of the landed gentry of Lithuania and Esthonia, of leaders in local and provincial administration as well as in the literary, social, and political life of the Russian capital. His own make-up combines in a remarkable degree the aristocratic virtues of the cavalier and the man of the world with the unbiased temper of the scientist, the democratic leanings of the rationalist philosopher, and the universally human sympathy of the mystic dreamer.

In 1902, as a youth of twenty-two, he took his degree of doctor of philosophy at the University of Vienna, having specialized in biology and geology. There followed years of travel and study in all European countries, alternating with periods of solitary meditation in the retreat of the ancestral estate of Rayküll in Esthonia. The years 1911 and 1912 were devoted to a trip around the world, the early part of 1914 to observations in Africa. The World War brought complete isolation in the Rayküll country seat, until the victorious drive of the German armies reëstablished connection with Central Europe. The Bolshevist revolution swept away all the family possessions, and the year 1919 saw Count Keyserling a refugee on German soil. Here he married Bismarck's only granddaughter; and in the following year, at forty years of age, he founded in Darmstadt, under the patronage of the former Grand Duke of Hesse, the "School of Wisdom," a loose intellectual organization analogous to the Platonic Academy, which is meant to form a rallying-point for free spirits seeking, in the midst of the wreck of all traditional forms of state and society, the foundations for a new life of the soul.

The key to this strangely complex, world-embracing character is to be found in the "Travel Diary of a Philosopher" (*Das Reisetagebuch eines Philosophen*), a comprehensive record of the impressions, emotions, and thoughts called forth by experiences in the Far East and North America during 1911 and 1912. Its first draft was finished just before the outbreak of the war; but it was revised, in part at least, in the midst of the war, and published in 1919. An English translation has been recently brought out in this country.[1]

"The shortest way to one's self is by a détour around the world"—this motto on the title-page aptly expresses the state of mind in which Count

[1] By Harcourt, Brace & Co.; now in its seventh impression.

Keyserling approached the various countries, the many different racial and national types, religions, philosophies of life with which his travels brought him in contact. From beginning to end this book is not so much an account of ethnological facts or social conditions as a reflex of successive inner experiences, the gradual and consistent self-unfolding of a spiritual personality. It should be read — so the author tells us himself — as a novel of the inner life.

Keyserling is indeed something of a Wilhelm Meister. His emotional and intellectual life is in constant flux. Transformation is a demand of his innermost nature. So he greets the beliefs and ideals of one people after another, as long as he dwells among them, as opportunities of identifying himself with them. Buddhism, Hinduism, Confucianism, Japanese self-mastery, American belief in progress, European striving for culture — of each and all he tries to see the positive side, the most fruitful part; in each and all he finds something helpful, some stimulus for heightening his own personality, for linking himself to what is more than personal, what is beyond all individual limitation.

A GERMAN VOICE OF HOPE

II

I doubt whether the spell of India — the first country where a longer sojourn was made by the world traveler — has ever, by a European, been put into words more impressive or genuine than in this notebook. By this I do not mean descriptions of scenery or art or people — the tropical exuberance of vegetation, the marvelous effects of light and shade, the wonders of temples and palaces, the inexhaustible variety and beauty of human types. To all these Keyserling does justice. But the real spell of India is reflected in his reaction to the vital energies of the Indian mind.

The fundamental quality of this mind Keyserling sees in its universality, its acceptance of life in all its forms and phases. For even the Buddhist negation of the ultimate reality of this world of appearances does not imply indifference to the forms in which this essentially unreal world happens to appear to us. The Buddhist conception of charity may be cited as one among many evidences of this spirit that forced themselves upon Keyserling.

"Christian charity," he says, "means the desire to do good to others; Buddhist charity means understanding and acceptance of others, each in his own place. For it is common Indian belief that every individual holds exactly the place where he belongs, whereto he has ascended or descended according to his own merit; every stage of his existence therefore has its inner justification and its own ideality. Christianity, as long as it was ascetic, rating the worldly life far below the monkish, would have liked to relegate all mankind to the monastery; Buddhism, although on principle still more hostile to the world than early Christianity, and although on principle rating the ascetic life as the highest of all, is far from condemning the lower on account of the higher. The flower, to the Buddhist, does not deny the leaf, the leaf does not deny the stalk and the root. To wish well to our fellow men does not mean to attempt to change all leaves into flowers, but to let them be leaves and love them as such. This superior charity shines forth from the faces of all Buddhist priests, however intellectually insignificant."

It is, however, not in this abstract realm of Buddhist doctrine that the universality of the Indian mind has found its widest manifestation. For Buddhism was after all a disintegrating influence in Hindu religion, comparable to the rôle played by Protestantism in the development of Christianity — a narrowing-down of all spiritual effort to one specific problem of individual redemption; and it has, as a church, ceased to be the religious interpreter of India. The catholicity of the Indian mind comes to light in forms of conduct and belief dominated by Brahmanism, the ancient but ever-youthful and honored popular religion.

With the avidity of a soul thirsting for the infinite, Keyserling drinks in all that he sees and hears of popular Hindu spirituality. Again and again he marvels at its wide sweep, its human breadth, its freedom from dogma, its sympathy with all living being. As its deepest source, however, he discerns the cardinal conception of the primacy of the psychic over the physical; and in this conception he finds an explanation for everything which in Hindu life appears strange and fantastic to the Western mind: the caste system, the exaltation of silence and meditation, the excesses of trance conditions, the indifference to material progress. But he also sees in it an important element of culture, the engrafting of which on our own mentality, overburdened with external things, would make for the rejuvenation of the Occidental world.

Two consequences of this Hindu insistence upon the primary reality of the psychic, and the derivative character of the physical, Keyserling singles out as of paramount significance for our own civilization: the Hindu ideal of perfection and the Hindu practice of Yoga.

The state of mind in itself and not what it accomplishes, not its relation to physical conditions, is according to Hindu belief the true measure of character. To be sure, this insight is not a monopoly of Hinduism. The Beatitudes of the Sermon on the Mount as well as Kant's definition of goodness mean essentially the same thing. But nowhere, Keyserling thinks, since the early days of Christianity has this principle had so deep a hold upon ideals of life as in the India of to-day; nowhere has it brought out so strikingly the fundamental difference between perfection and progress. The Hindu believes whole-heartedly in perfection, but only qualifiedly in progress. He believes that to each individual there is assigned in the universal scheme of things an individual sphere of outward activity within which he may reach perfection, but which it would be wrong to

A GERMAN VOICE OF HOPE

transcend. He believes that a lower state perfectly fulfilled is nearer to the Godhead than a higher state imperfectly fulfilled. At the same time, he believes that this very restriction of individual perfection to specific spheres established by an over-individual power may, through reincarnation, lead to individual progress beyond these spheres. He who has faithfully and with complete self-surrender lived out the tasks of a lower form of life will be reincarnated in a higher form; and thus there is indeed an ascending line of spirits spread through the universe.

Thoughts like these naturally appeal to a man of Keyserling's spiritual bent. To him the Hindu ideal of perfection appears indeed, theoretically at least, as the very climax of human wisdom. And he is willing to accept its practical consequences even in so extreme a case as that of the hermit saint who in absolute detachment and absolute silence spends his years of meditation on the banks of the Ganges, worshipped by the whole countryside. For this man is to him an embodiment of the profound truth that it is not *doing*—not even doing good — that counts, but only and exclusively *being:* that is, the state of mind in which one does or does not, as the case may be.

Since happiness and unhappiness entirely depend on this inner state, even the most favorable change of outward conditions does not accomplish anything truly essential. To do good is a wise rule of conduct, not so much for the sake of the beneficiaries as for the sake of the benefactors. The beneficiaries indeed are very often inwardly harmed by these very acts; they are confirmed by them in their selfishness, they are hampered in the necessary task of becoming free from themselves. The benefactors themselves, on the other hand, are helped by these acts toward their inner freedom. Complete freedom from self, however, the highest goal, is best typified by such an existence as that of the hermit saint by the Ganges. He lives as an example of what others strive for, a life raised above both egoism and altruism; and such an example is worth more than any quantity of good acts.

With equal open-mindedness and sympathetic understanding Count Keyserling enters into the second fundamental Hindu conception, the practice of Yoga, the training of the will by ever-repeated concentration upon its higher possibilities. He is not blind to the fact that this practice is often perverted from its true purpose; that in-

A GERMAN VOICE OF HOPE

stead of leading to the freeing from selfish desires it often leads to the very opposite: to the concentration of the mind upon nothing but itself, and thence to individual self-glorification and self-adulation. But that an immense service has been rendered by this practice to all higher life in India seems to him beyond question. He has tried it himself and found it so useful that he would advocate its being made an integral part of all education everywhere.

Can there be any doubt that the three essentials of Yoga practice — heightening the power of concentration, putting a stop to the vagaries of automatic soul-action by fixing one's mind upon its deepest sources of strength, vitalizing psychic processes the prevalence of which will increase the soul's efficacy — are all of them calculated to make a man master of his soul in the same sense in which an athlete has become master of his body? These exercises, then, trivial as they may appear to the superficial observer, may indeed be made most powerful instruments in the spiritualization of a man's whole being, in raising him to a new and higher level of consciousness. This higher level of consciousness, a chronic state of inspiration, so to speak, induced by calling up the innermost and essential energies of the subconscious self, is the avowed goal of all Hindu philosophy. The need of this in our present age, estranged from the religious faith of former centuries, harassed by national passions, overwrought by humdrum toil, material greed, and sensual excitement, is so self-evident that any rational help for attaining to it must be welcomed. Keyserling is convinced that among all the helps offered for a similar purpose from many quarters the Hindu call to the deep is the most rational [1] and the most momentous; he sees in the reception of India's message by Western civilization a real hope of restoring Europe to her spiritual equilibrium.

These are some Diary entries from Benares:

"The great superiority of India over the Occident consists in the fundamental insight that true culture cannot be acquired by expansion, but only by deepening of one's self; that the process of deepening is necessarily a process of concentration. Hindu philosophy, so-called, does not rest upon what we understand by thinking. Witness the traditional Hindu method of instruction, as

[1] For myself, I confess that I do not see its rationality. But I feel its inspirational quality.

described in the Upanishads. When the pupil raises a question, the teacher does not answer straight, but simply says: 'Come and live with me for ten years.' And during these ten years he does not instruct him as we understand the word; he gives him some maxim for meditation. The pupil is not to criticize it, analyze it, develop it; he is to sink himself in it until his whole soul has been completely suffused by it. Kant used to say to his students: 'I am not going to teach you a particular system of philosophy, I am going to teach you how to think.' Just that is what the Hindu Guru does not teach his pupil. Instead, he tries to help him to reach a new level of consciousness, through transformation of his psychic organism to get beyond the limits set to ordinary human experience.

"The Hindus, one might say, have replaced the static conception of knowledge by a dynamic one. Sooner or later we also shall come to see that knowledge of the essence of things is not to be attained by however far-reaching a perfection of our critical faculties, not through however exhaustive an analysis of our consciousness as it is, but only through the evoking from the depths of our being of a new and higher form of consciousness. Man must lift himself above his secular instrument of knowledge, he must reach out beyond the biological limits the classic definition of which is contained in Kant's *Critiques;* he must outgrow his present measure; his consciousness, instead of clinging to the surface, must mirror the spirit of the deep which is the psychic foundation of its whole being. This higher development has begun in India, hence the wonders of Hindu insight into the essence of things. It is for us to carry this development further.

"This is the path, the only one, that leads beyond our present state. We need not renounce any of our intellectual achievements. The breadth of horizon acquired by the modern mind is not to be reduced. The enormous differentiation of our faculties is a gain and must be maintained. The task is to make all these differentiated faculties subservient to our inmost central being. If we succeed in this, we shall have made ourselves types of a new and higher humanity."

It is a pity that Count Keyserling did not see India after the Gandhi movement had stirred all classes of the nation to a new and unprecedented spiritual effort. The last days, however, of his Indian sojourn were devoted to a stay with the

A GERMAN VOICE OF HOPE

other great representative of modern Hindu culture, Rabindranath Tagore. Of an evening spent at his house, listening to native musicians, he says:

"Indian music is only another, richer, and fuller expression of Indian wisdom. He who wishes to understand it must have realized his own self, must know that the individual is only a fleeting tone in the great world-symphony, that everything belongs together, that nothing can be isolated, and that every objective existence is only the glimpse of a moment in the current of mysterious ever-flowing life. He must know that all phenomena are only a reflection of the invisible Being, and that our redemption lies in anchoring our consciousness in this Being. Tagore himself impressed me as a visitor from that higher region. Never perhaps have I seen so much spirituality concentrated in a human form."

III

It is not easy to state briefly [1] what spiritual harvest Count Keyserling gathered from his contact with the two other great Asiatic civilizations:

---

[1] Perhaps I should say that in this whole essay I have taken the liberty of condensing and in a way vulgarizing Keyserling's highly metaphysical and often elusive language.

the Chinese and the Japanese. Certain it is that he entered into both of them with the same divinatory understanding, the same capacity for reproducing in himself states of mind traditionally not his own, which had been such a help to him in fathoming the Hindu soul.

What in China seems to have impressed him more than anything else is the settled popular belief in the fundamental harmony between the moral world and the physical, and the serene submission to the natural order of things resulting from this belief. The Chinaman, as he appears in this Diary, is the very embodiment of proper adjustment to existing conditions. His is a static world, but this static world contains a wealth of refinement, of beauty, of happiness, of wisdom, such as the restless striving of the Occidental mind rarely brings about. Neither Confucius nor Lao-tsze distinguishes, as most European thinkers have done, between the inexorableness of matter and spiritual freedom; to them there is nothing but nature — nature living out a moral process, and therefore easily accessible to moral appeals and motives from the human end of it. Whereas Christianity and Western philosophy challenge man to rise above the world of the senses into the

A GERMAN VOICE OF HOPE

free realm of the spirit, Confucianism counsels man to adapt himself to the all-embracing law of nature. The former inspire us to dare the impossible, the latter teaches how to accomplish the possible. Instead of the Kantian imperative "Thou shalt," Confucius holds out to his followers an alluring "Thou wilt." Instead of addressing himself to the chosen few, he appeals to the multitude of average men. Obviously Confucianism does not lead to the cultivation of highly differentiated individualities, but it does lead to a mass morality of an extraordinarily high order, perhaps the highest in existence.

Two types of Chinese character as described by Keyserling — the peasant and the high official — may serve to illustrate the effect of such principles upon human conduct. This is what the Diary has to say about the Chinese peasant in Shantung Province or the basin of the Yangtze River:

"Nowhere have I seen such impressive pictures of country existence as on this trip through the interior of China. The whole soil is under cultivation, carefully enriched, neatly and skillfully tilled, reaching up to the highest crests of the hills, which slope down, like the pyramids of

Egypt, in artificial terraces. The villages, built of clay and surrounded by clay walls, appear as integral forms of the landscape; so little are they set off from the brownish background. All over the wide plain the peasants are at work, methodical, deliberate, serene; the blue of their frocks is as necessary a part of the picture as the green of the fields or the glaring yellow of the dried-up river-beds. But this whole plain is also one immense graveyard. Hardly an acre that does not contain numerous burial mounds; again and again the ploughman is compelled to wind his way around the memorial tablets. No other peasantry creates so strong an impression of autochthonousness. Here all life and all death are absorbed by the ancestral soil. Man belongs to it, not it to man; permanently entailed, it never releases its children. Be the increase of their number ever so large, they remain upon the soil, forcing its chary returns by ever more assiduous toil. In death they return confidently to the bosom of their common Mother. There they live forever, and the glebe exhales their spirit to reward the descendants for faithfulness in work or to chastise them for neglect of duty. For the responsibility of the peasant is great. He is the foundation of

A GERMAN VOICE OF HOPE

the whole order of the world. If he does not live up to his duty, then heaven and earth are shaken, and the whole moral order is out of joint. But if the peasant's life is as it should be, then nature also will be in a friendly mood, and the long-looked-for rain or sunshine will come."

And this is from the notes on a company of viceroys, governors, and other high officials ousted by the revolution, whom Keyserling met as exiles at the then German port of Tsingtau:

"These men are superior types of humanity, whatever they may have been as officials. Not alone because they are masters of their exterior fate, at present so distressing. They are above their own thoughts, their actions, their selves; not in the manner of the Yogi, who has lifted himself above the realm of phenomena, but in the manner of the man of the world who in the midst of the affairs in which he partakes has preserved his inner freedom. In India the people as people had disappointed me; they are less than their thoughts. Their highest and profoundest being has found expression in abstract knowledge; and the living Hindus are for the most part not incarnations but actors of their striving for the ideal. The Chinese intellectuals are more than their wisdom. They live Confucianism. What I looked upon as a theoretical postulate is to them the natural form of their existence. To all these statesmen it seemed self-evident that the State rests on a moral basis, that politics is the practical expression of ethics, and justice the normal outgrowth of benevolence. Our own political culture is something of an external garment; it is the result of a system which forces the individual to act correctly; it has nothing to do with the soul life. The political culture of the Chinese rests upon the cultivation of this very thing, the inner life. And if we remember that the Chinese Empire has been ruled for thousands of years hardly worse than modern Europe, without much of an administrative mechanism automatically keeping people in order, solely through the moral qualifications of its citizens, one must admit that the average level of moral culture among the Chinese intellectuals must be remarkably high. Remarkably high it surely was with the intellectuals with whom I came in contact. . . . They consider us moral barbarians. Our systems, they admitted, were admirable; but what of the men and their fundamental character? I fear these gentlemen are right. Our political systems are functioning with precision. But we are inferior to our systems; the Chinese are superior to theirs. That is the result of Confucian education."

To sum up. China, Imperial China (for the Chinese Republic is still a thing of doubtful character and uncertain prospects), has given to mankind a highly valuable type of collective moral strength, based upon a view of the world of striking unity and consistency. According to this view the moral law and the physical law belong to the selfsame all-embracing system of terrestrial existence. Identical norms regulate moral conduct, the sequence of the seasons, the recurrent changes of night and day. There is one great living whole which contains in itself the human and the non-human, the organic and the inorganic, the natural and the moral, as component parts of a higher harmony. The moral element, however, is the primary element. Therefore nature runs the risk of sinking back into chaos when men neglect their natural duties; when the fathers are no good fathers, husbands no good husbands, princes no good princes, subjects no good subjects; when the five heavenly virtues — justice, magnanimity, courteousness, insight, loyalty — are not assiduously practised. As soon, however, as the moral law is upheld, everything else automatically sets itself right. In this fundamental trust in moral principle lies China's greatness. "China has remained great, although she hardly ever was a great political power, and although in war she has almost always been defeated. China will remain great, even if she should be divided up among other nations."

It would seem that the liberal-conservative Keyserling was better qualified to appreciate Chinese civilization than the radical Bertrand Russell, who from his recent sojourn in Peking brought back as his chief impression the conviction that the sacrifice of the individual to the social order is the curse of all Chinese life. Keyserling, indeed, like Bertrand Russell, clearly sees that the cultivation of mass morality entails the danger of leveling all individuals down to the standard of the average. But, being temperamentally given to seeking out the positive side of things, he discounts this defect of Chinese culture in comparison with the inestimable benefits which all mankind may derive from the Chinese principle that ethics is the only safe basis of conduct in all human affairs, private and public, national and international.

A GERMAN VOICE OF HOPE

IV

What is it that in Japan impressed our traveler as containing a message of world import? Many of his observations are in line with what other writers, from Lafcadio Hearn on, have told us about Japanese landscape, Japanese feeling for nature, the exquisiteness of Japanese art, the charm of Japanese women, and the depth of Japanese patriotism. One contribution, however, of Keyserling's to the understanding of Japanese character seems to me to outweigh all the rest.

He objects to the word "imitative" as applied to it. No, the Japanese are not imitators — they are exploiters, appropriators, adapters. Without having the depth of the Hindu absorption in the infinite, they have evolved from Buddhism a religion of superlative heroism. Without having an artistic originality and productiveness equal to that of the Chinese, they have, by closest observation and assimilation of Chinese models, in many ways outdistanced Chinese art. Without having invented any of the methods of modern strategy, they have applied them with such supreme skill as to shatter the military strength of the vast Russian Empire. Theirs is a civilization of mental tactics; the fit symbol of their whole national life is their method of wrestling, the jujutsu. As the Japanese wrestler watches every play of muscle, every fleeting facial expression, every involuntary motion on the part of his opponent, and instantaneously adapts his own movements thereto, so the Japanese as a nation are constantly on the alert in trying to find out what in other national cultures is either strikingly beneficial or strikingly harmful, so as to avoid or adopt similar characteristics or states of mind as quickly as possible. They are fully abreast in this respect with the progressive nations of Europe.

V

So Japan forms intellectually as well as geographically a fitting transition stage to the last protracted stay in Count Keyserling's flight around the civilizations of the globe: the United States of America. And here the observer of the past turns into a prophet of the future.

His first pilgrimage is to the giants of the Mariposa forest. He greets them with enthusiasm as messengers of the spirit of the West: exuberant nature, which in India produces a promiscuous,

A GERMAN VOICE OF HOPE

bewildering jungle, creates on American soil the mighty, sovereign sequoia, sharply outlined, rivalry-defying, soaring skyward — what a symbol of American individualism! What an encouragement to the Occidental state of mind in general! For it is the spirit of modern Occidental Europe, carried to its furthest limit, which Keyserling sees everywhere in the United States, from his first sight of the Golden Gate to his passing the Statue of Liberty, homeward bound.

Being by temper and tradition a conservative, and having just steeped himself in the conceptions and ideals of the timeless, immutable East, he has a keen eye for the defects and dangers of a society the very essence of which is fluidity and absorption in the moment. The modern individual in general, and the modern American in particular, only too often is a fanatic of progress. There is nothing definitive for him; everything is but a stepping-stone toward something else; instead of identifying himself, like the Hindu, with a permanent task and striving for perfection in it, he thinks of it as a rôle temporarily assumed, and the change of rôles quite as much as the acting of them is what gives zest to his life. The same fanaticism of progress is responsible for many other defects and dangers of modern European, and particularly American, life: its prevailing materialism, its lack of true culture, the enslaving influence of machinery, the impoverishment of the soul by what is called success. Keyserling's notes are full of serious observations on these evils.

And yet, that first vision of American greatness which came to him at the sight of the giant sequoias in the Mariposa forest was not a fleeting dream. It stands by him as he crosses the country; it upholds him in Chicago and New York; it gives to the last chapters of his book the character of a strikingly hopeful finale. All the evils mentioned and many others are to Keyserling after all but necessary concomitants of a comprehensive movement essentially forward and upward: the movement from a democracy of material wealth toward a new aristocracy of the spirit.

Even Europe has been transformed during the last hundred years by the typically Western spirit of individual initiative. In many ways this spirit has acted as a destroyer. It has broken up inherited allegiances, undermined religious beliefs, subverted moral systems, disintegrated governments, leveled down social distinctions, sacrificed beauty to utility, commercialized and barbarized the soul. But it has also freed from bondage, bettered social conditions, increased popular health, brought forth great leaders, strengthened the will, created a new idealism, throughout Europe. Present-day America, however, is the classic soil of this spirit of individual initiative; here its effects have been unparalleled, both for good and for ill. As for the latter, it is hardly necessary to dwell on the avalanches of ugliness with which individual enterprise has covered the country; or on the singular form of barbarism to which it has led by producing a class of inordinately rich totally unable to enjoy their riches æsthetically; or on any other distortions of human nature for which it has been responsible. The point is that Keyserling, while not ignoring these distortions, keeps his gaze steadily fixed on the positive contribution which this intensely individualized American society has made to the world's advancement, and on the prospects which it holds in store for the future.

America, Keyserling thinks, is of all countries the country where a higher type of the Occidental temper is in the making.

In the first place, the Occidental conception of

strife as a fundamental form of human existence has in America been modified by a peculiarly optimistic and humane tinge. The American rightly feels that the conditions under which he lives are such that he can enter the strife with a good chance of winning out. This gives to American business competition a certain charm of daring adventure, hiding the bald egotism which underlies it after all. And, by giving larger scope to the principle of fair play, it takes away from the struggles of industrial life, violent as these struggles may occasionally be, much of the bitter and chronic hatred which in Europe poisons the relations between Capital and Labor. These are, however, not the only instances of the American's good-natured acceptance of fight as a part of the day's work; the national games, college rivalries, the contest of political parties — all have this same aspect of boyish exuberance and delight in trying one's limbs, literally and metaphorically. In fact, the whole history of the settlement of the continent and the opening-up of vast areas to civilized life has been one continuous testimony to the optimism of a people spoiling for a good fight. What this means for the future of higher culture in America, it is hard to overestimate.

A GERMAN VOICE OF HOPE

The optimistic and frankly condoning attitude toward material wealth, so characteristic of American life, is another point in which America is carrying forward tendencies that have long been at work in Europe, and is bringing them to their full fruition. Early Christianity was, theoretically at least, a religion for the poor and an enemy of riches. Luther reasserted the dignity of secular pursuits; Calvin made worldly efficiency a touchstone of spiritual selectness. But in America for the first time has worldly success been sanctified, not only by popular opinion, but by the churches as well. With the exception of the Salvation Army, there is indeed no Protestant church in America which did not make its primary appeal to the well-to-do, and was not chiefly supported by them; and the two most modern and particularly active sects, Christian Science and New Thought, avowedly cultivate a state of mind that makes for a happy and prosperous material existence. Who would deny that revolting consequences have arisen from this union of Church and Mammon? But who would not also agree with Count Keyserling that it is after all a good symptom when rich men are beginning habitually to supplement their quest for the goods of this world by the striving for ideals? Where wealth, as is the case in America, is looked upon by the rich themselves as carrying with it the obligation to provide for the things of the spirit, the rise of an intellectual aristocracy seems assured.

Is it fanciful to believe with Keyserling that its rise is also being prepared by the present rapid strides in substituting machinery for human labor, or by the extraordinary advances in the organization on a large scale of all the agencies catering to the daily needs of life? Perhaps he is a little too confident that the energy released by these changes will really be put in the service of the spirit. One aspect, however, of his augury of the future we can accept without reserve and whole-heartedly: the new aristocracy of the spirit, destined to bring about a golden age of American culture, will recruit itself largely from the ranks of the intelligent, moderately well-to-do freemen — farmers, mechanics, village storekeepers, engineers — who constitute after all the vast majority and the true strength of the American people. In them the Occidental spirit of individual initiative has found representative types of rare sturdiness and efficiency; and in the fluid state of the society of which they are a part there is nothing to hinder their sons and daughters from rising, externally as well as internally, to higher strata. Of this type is peculiarly true what Keyserling says of the American in general: "Aus ihm kann noch alles werden" (in him there is the making of everything).

VI

The Hindu ideal of individual perfection within a given limit, Chinese belief in the harmony between the moral and the physical order, Japanese genius for intellectual exploitation, American power of individual initiative — these, unsatisfactory as all such formulas are, may be said to constitute the mental harvest which Keyserling brought back from his trip around the world, a harvest of particular value to a people trying to reconstruct its life upon a new moral basis.

More valuable, however, than any of these individual acquisitions was to him and is to us the fact that his very delving into the differences of national types and beliefs strengthened and vivified his feeling of the solidarity and common humanity of these different peoples, and thus gave him something of that over-individual consciousness which he had set out to attain. This feeling upheld and inspired him when, in the midst of the World War, on his lonely estate in Esthonia, he set to work digesting and revising his travel notes. And ever since he has devoted himself to the spreading of this gospel of a new world-consciousness, a world-consciousness based not upon illusive notions of a supposed equality of national types, but upon exact knowledge of their differences and of their peculiar contributions to the common stock of humanity. Poor, embittered, down-trodden Germany is the land where this message at the present time is perhaps needed most, but it is needed everywhere. And, wherever it is heard, it cannot fail to bring a new hope for the future.

"We are coming" — these are among the closing words of this remarkable book — "We are coming to a broadening of the generally human basis of our life such as was never known before, and at the same time to a deepening and intensifying of every individual racial tendency equally unparalleled. While formerly there was the alternative, nationalism or cosmopolitanism, there will henceforth be a mutual penetration of the two. The different types of culture and belief will come to respect each other as necessary complements of

A GERMAN VOICE OF HOPE

each other. The former 'He or I' will more and more be transformed into a conscious and deliberate 'We.' And this will take place almost independently of all good will, because the life of the world is itself a connected whole. Already, in science, in money, in economic interdependence, foundations have been laid on the basis of which mutual agreement is inevitable; soon the same will be the case in legal relations. These objective realizations of internationalism, on their part, react upon the subjective side, the states of mind. More and more leading minds are renouncing all exclusiveness of national culture. The international solidarity of Labor is daily becoming more powerful. On some day of grace all humanity will feel as one, in spite of all conflicts and contrasts.

"To help in bringing about this blessed day and this better world — that, and not the Occidentalization of the rest of the globe, is the mission of us Occidentals. It is the mission of the West to put into practice what the East, and especially India, has first understood as a theoretical command."

III

GERMAN CHARACTER AND THE GERMAN–AMERICAN
(1926)

IT is natural that the collapse of German political power, and the violent and unreasonable defamations of everything German which in this country resulted from the war, should have brought to German-Americans much distress, much searching of the heart, and much groping about for the true sources of German greatness and for the elements in German character from which a new era of high national culture may be hoped for. The following reflections may be considered as an individual reflex of this general state of mind.

I

I agree with two of the most distinguished German writers of to-day, Count Keyserling and Thomas Mann, that the Germans are not, in the true sense, a political nation. Only I do not, like them, see in this a title of honor, but an unfortunate limitation of German character. The whole course of German history has been a tragic confirmation of this fact. There have not been absent individual political achievements of high merit. I am thinking of the constitutions of the mediæval free cities, the organization of the Prussian State under Frederick the Great, the reform legislation of Stein and Hardenberg, the transformation by Bismarck of a loose federation of states (*Staatenbund*) into a centralized state-confederacy (*Bundesstaat*), the model administration of the German cities of to-day. But only in rare moments of high distress or high enthusiasm has the whole nation been united in common action. The sober, persistent work in building up a free national commonwealth, such as the English people has engaged in for centuries, the German people has hardly known.

How erratic, for the most part, was the foreign policy of the mediæval German Empire. What a waste of human material and mental energy was entailed in the oft-repeated crossing of the Alps by German armies for the sake of winning the Roman crown, the foolish attempt to crush the Lombard city-republics, the fantastic designs to extend German sovereignty even as far as Sicily. To speak, as has been frequently done by German historians, with patriotic fervor, of these high-flown imperialistic schemes of the Ottos, Fredericks, and Henrys, to consider them evidences of noble national aspirations, is a piece of strange political aberration. Far from having added to national power and prosperity, this fantastic policy of conquest has harmed the Empire both at home and abroad; at home, through the delegation of sovereign rights to the higher nobility, forced upon the Emperors thereby, and the consequent weakening of the central power; abroad, through the kindling of bitter national hatreds and resentments. The political disintegration and isolation of Germany, then, at the end of the Middle Ages were the natural result of centuries of neglect of what should have been the main concern of the ruling classes — the knighthood and the free cities: the creation of national institutions which would have made possible habitual coöperation of all the estates of the Empire and habitual compromise between class interests and national tasks.

The Reformation of the sixteenth century seemed for a time to carry the whole German people with it, urged on by a wave of high moral enthusiasm. When Luther, at the Diet of Worms, upheld freedom of conscience in the face of the most formidable array of Church and State authority, the heart of Germany was with him. Never before in German history had there arisen a national hero like him; never before had there been a moment of equally portentous promises and possibilities. On Luther's side stood the most enlightened and influential of the princes, and a large part of the knighthood; the free cities greeted him as a champion in their fight against episcopal encroachments upon their privileges; the peasants divined in him the deliverer from social injustice and serfdom. What might not have been achieved, if all friends of reform had stood together, if all party demands and class interests had been merged in one great stream of the people's cause, if the creation of a great free commonwealth, such as hovered before Hutten's imagination, had become the watchword of all. It was the German lack of political instinct which spoiled this opportunity. Each class by itself — the peasants, the knights, the cities, the territorial princes — clung after all to its own special interests. And from the wild civil wars which resulted from the conflict of these interests there arose at last the princely absolutism of the seventeenth century as the only firm, dominant political power — a lamentable outcome of a movement which had set in with the highest hopes for the freedom of the individual in matters of State as well as of Church.

Among the absolute monarchies which, from the Thirty Years' War on, overruled private as well as public existence in Germany, the Brandenburg-Prussian State unquestionably held a place of exceptional worth. The Hohenzollern princes, from the Great Elector to Frederick the Great, were in their way perfect types of governmental methods consecrated to the public welfare. Allegiance to duty, sense of order, economy, honesty, methodical care of popular education and prosperity, have become through them permanent characteristics of German officialdom. But an unloosening of common political activities, a delivery of popular political forces, was the last thing for which the Hohenzollerns stood. Something hard, rigid, class-bound, inheres in every contribution of theirs to public progress. The collapse of this whole elaborate state-machinery under the assault of the Napoleonic armies, inspired with the rhetoric of great national ideals, however illusive, revealed its inner torpidity and lack of soul.

The rising of 1813 brought once more, like the sixteenth-century Reformation, one of those great historical moments when a people carried away by one mighty feeling and united by one supreme aim seems capable of achieving the impossible. For the German youth which then rallied to the colors was impelled with the determination, not only to drive the foreign conqueror from the ancestral soil, but also to create a new Germany, a Germany transformed from a geographical term comprising an ill-assorted conglomeration of more or less despotic governments into a great national body of free commonwealths. But again, as in the time of the Reformation, the great moment passed without leaving permanent results. As soon as the victory over the foreign enemy was achieved, the old political short-sightedness, the old distrust of free coöperation of all classes, asserted its baneful sway. A dull, spiritless bureaucracy, which had learned nothing from the popular rising, and which had forgotten all the evils of the past, succeeded for decades in repressing all liberal thought and attempts at reform, outlawed and persecuted the noblest patriots and most distinguished men of letters, and attempted to force a nation, raised through the classic achievements of German philosophy, literature, and music to the highest level of spirituality, back into the humiliating fetters of the ancient régime. And when, in spite of all this, in the Revolution of 1848 the new spirit triumphantly broke forth and irresistibly swept away all impeding barriers, it was again not, as so often has been asserted, the inexperienced idealism of the Frankfort Parliament, but the political obtuseness of the governmental classes, and their inability to harness and direct the popular idealism as a driving force in creating a new Empire, which robbed even this noblest "Springtime of Nations" of its best fruits.

The final unification of Germany in the Hohenzollern Empire of 1871 was undoubtedly a remarkable achievement of Bismarckian diplomacy; and yet even this achievement of the greatest German statesman lacked the crowning merit of true political wisdom. Bismarck's own internal policy suffered from two fundamental defects: his undervaluation of the moral strength of the Catholic Church and his unconditional condemnation of Social-Democracy. The coercive measures of the so-called Kulturkampf—the incarceration of bishops, the wholesale suspension of Catholic priests, the expulsion of the Jesuits and other religious orders—outraged the feelings of the Catholic population, one of the staunchest and most stalwart sections of the whole German people, and estranged it from allegiance to the Empire in the very first years of its existence. And the official denunciation and degradation of the Social-Democratic Party, a party led by men of such moderation and insight as Bebel and Liebknecht, into a band of intractable traitors and "enemies of the Empire," with whom no compromise could be thought of, instilled a poison into all German political life of the last fifty years which no amount of paternal workingmen's legislation has been able to counteract.

Particularly disastrous in the further course of the Wilhelminian era came to be the political shortcomings of the German bourgeoisie. If the German bourgeoisie in political matters had had only one tenth of the insight it betrayed in commercial and industrial organization, it would have recognized the necessity of forming with the Social-Democrats a solid party of opposition, strong enough in internal affairs to guard parliamentary rights, and in European and colonial questions to curb the aimlessly provoking bravado of the imperial policy. The fact that, with the exception of the numerically inconsequential Progressive Party, the German bourgeoisie, from fear of the Social-Democrats, delivered itself up hand and foot to the reactionary jingoism of the ultra-nationalists seems to me in the tragedy of the last decades to form a particularly tragic episode; at any rate, it is another striking illustration of how little instinctive sense for political fundamentals the average German possesses, and how little we are justified in holding up German political experiments as models to be followed by other nations. A noteworthy exception to this is found in the lack of corruption in the German civil service and the nonpartisan objectivity of German municipal administration — recognized the world over as shining examples of honesty, efficiency, and common sense.

II

If then — to sum up all the foregoing — the peculiar virtue of the German does not lie in his qualification for national politics, where may we look for the traits in which he is distinguished from other national types and perhaps superior to them? To say it in a word: in the depth of the individual personality. A few manifestations of this side of German character may briefly be considered. "Not a great nation, only great men" — thus Heinrich Mann, the counterpart of his brother Thomas, has characterized Germany. I take the part of Heinrich against his brother [1] by briefly pointing out in what special sense the great men of German history have been lonely men, how little they owed to the masses, how deeply they were anchored in themselves.

From Luther to Nietzsche there extends a long chain of men who, for pronounced subjectivity, for defiant independence from the crowd spirit, and for intensity of inner strength, hardly have their equals. At the head of them Luther himself, the hero of the "Here I stand; I cannot do otherwise"; the man of ironic contempt of the world which, at the very height of his activity, made him say: "I trust that in course of time my books will be forgotten in the dust, especially what good through the grace of God they may contain"; the

[1] It is gratifying to note that, in spite of his indifference to politics, Thomas Mann himself has openly come out for the Republic.

unswerving apostle of faith who drove away all attacks of doubt and despondency with the word: "The Lord has said He would dwell in the gloom and has made the darkness His tent." Johann Sebastian Bach, who, from the modest round of his Leipzig organist life, called forth artistic creations in which all suffering, all longing, all dumb striving for light and freedom, seem transformed into a world raised above all limitations of reality, a world of eternal suns and heavenly bliss. Klopstock, who in an epoch of weakly and petty sentiments dared "to think creation's thought anew"; who pierced the commonplace barriers of his surroundings with the trumpet sound of his own full, generous personality; who inspired a generation crushed under the weight of political oppression with the prophetic word:

> *Not forever crusheth it! Free, O Germans,*
> *Are you to be! But a century more*
> *And it is done, and there rules*
> *Reason's right over sword's right.*

Lessing, the lonely champion of genuine individuality and inner truthfulness; lacking every support or background of a living literary tradition; conquering every inch of intellectual territory by himself; pointing to new paths in æsthetic criticism, in dramatic production, in religious speculation; in his whole reformatory activity guided by the thought which he for the first time expressed in some youthful album verses:

> *How soon 't will be until the sham*
> *Of life is gone for me!*
> *Why should my name*
> *Be known to fame*
> *And to posterity,*
> *If only I with certainty*
> *Know who I am!*

and for the last time in the last words of his last work: "Is not all eternity mine?" Kant, the self-centred thinker, who — without any personal contact with the actual world in its wider aspects, confined throughout his life to the narrow boundaries of an isolated provincial town — through mere reasoning created a world in which sensuous experience appears as product of the mind, and in which the moral life is ruled by the principle: "Thou canst, for thou shalt"; the retiring scholar, who in the midst of an age bristling in arms clung to the idea of "permanent peace," not dreaming about it as a utopia, but setting it forth as a necessary consequence of a democratized Europe. Schiller, who not only, as a youth, hurled flaming words against class tyranny and princely absolutism, but whose whole lifework and highest artistic achievements were inspired by the desire to replace the humdrum, mechanized, fragmentary existence of the despotic state by a free, creative humanism, developing all vital powers and leading to totality of character. Goethe, whose world-wide activity essentially bore the signature of his own dictum: "Highest bliss of human kind rests after all in personality"; who, at the end of the "Classical Walpurgis Night," when the shades are recalled from their brief earthly existence, lets only Helena and the leader of the chorus return to the conscious life of the Beyond, while the mass of the chorus is dissolved into the elements of earth and air. Fichte, who, during the occupation of Berlin by the French, writes to a friend: "People here are near despair, and it is hard to see what will become of us during the coming winter if these guests do not leave us. I, locked up in a lonely garden-house, guard myself as well as I can lest a sound of that despair or of the insults by which it is caused penetrate across my threshold; for I must retain the freedom of my spirit to think out the principles of a better order of things"; and who in this state of mind sets himself to writing his "Ad-

GERMAN CHARACTER

dresses to the German Nation," the intellectual call-to-arms against the foreign oppression. Heinrich von Kleist, who, driven about by fate, ignored or misjudged even by the best of his people, consumes himself in passionate attempts to find inner poise and control of his instincts, until at last he leaves to his indifferent contemporaries immortal poetic embodiments of his own self. Hebbel, the stubborn self-willed Frisian, who condenses his opposition to traditional morality into the word: "Not all the Ten Commandments whip a man forward as vehemently as do his own youthful follies"; and whose life-work is that of a man who, as it were, with his teeth set and his eyes closed sets about to hammer out of the quarry of the past a new feeling of humanity and a new form of dramatic art. Richard Wagner, who with titanic self-reliance and boundless contempt for people and opinions that stand in his way, in a much higher sense than Hebbel, conquers for the German drama a new domain of astounding emotional effects. Bismarck, who asserted that a wave of popularity always made him doubtful of himself, and who was never more himself than when facing a hostile majority either in the old Frankfort Bundestag or in the Prussian

Landtag or in the diplomatic concert of Europe. Carl Schurz, who not only in Germany, single-handed, defied political tyranny by rescuing, at the risk of his own life, a noble apostle of freedom from death behind prison walls, but who in this country also stood only too often alone as unflinchingly opposed to any kind of party dictation in matters of principle. And finally Nietzsche, the social-aristocrat, for whom the masses had interest only in three respects: "first as dimmed copies of the great men, printed on poor paper and from worn-out plates; secondly as opposition to the great; and finally as instruments of the great — for the rest, may the Devil and statistics take them"; the recluse of Sils-Maria, who feels himself "exiled from father- and mother-lands" and seeks only his "children-land, the undiscovered one in the farthest sea," in order to "atone to his children" for his being his "forefathers' child"; the prophet of the Superman who may say of himself: "I walk among men as fragments of the future, that future which I see. And all my desire and striving is only this: to bring together and form into a whole what is fragment."

What a gallery — and it might easily be doubled and trebled — what a gallery of heads, of sharply chiseled individuals, personalities rooted in themselves, to whom the bringing into play, the heightening and broadening, of their own self is an inner necessity, and who, unconcerned about the opinion of the crowd, charmed against misjudgment and slander, with the whole weight of men singled out by fate, throw themselves into their appointed task. Truly in men like these the politically sterile Germany has brought forth cultural values which benefit all striving men in all countries — shining examples of the victorious spirit of all times.

III

If thus the most significant German personalities have, for the most part, achieved their highest either apart from the masses or in opposition to them, the average German seems to me to possess in an unusual degree the capacity to draw inner profit from outward conditions.

What I mean hereby may be illustrated by the fact that in no country of the world, with the exception perhaps of China, is the value of intellectual training so generally recognized as in Germany. Nowhere in Europe or America does scholarship as such, irrespective of its practical utility, enjoy a social prestige so widely spread. Nowhere is the title of professor so universally and instinctively honored. Nowhere do school questions — the children's marks in the semestral examinations, their promotions from one form to another — play such a part in family life. Nowhere are the children so early taught to make a choice for their professional career; nowhere do they learn so early to have respect for their intellectual superiors. To be sure, all this is connected with the less wholesome aspects of German life: on the one hand with the harshness of the struggle for existence and the economic necessity of working up from narrow conditions; on the other with a certain submissiveness of German character which is itself a consequence of these narrow conditions. On the whole, however, we may say that this instinctive recognition of intellectual values imparts even to the average German life deeper substance and more earnest aspiration than is to be found in the average life of most other countries. That there is mixed up with this a good deal of half-knowing and loose thinking cannot be denied. I doubt, for instance, whether the thousands of German students who within the last decade have been carried away by Oswald Spengler's *Decay of the Occident* have got from it more than a vague notion of the worthlessness of all previous historical writing and a confused conception of a certain parallelism in the development of national cultures. But the mere fact that such a book, the ponderous product of an immense learning and of an astounding power of fantastic combination of facts, which on almost every page confronts the critical reader with doubts and conundrums, should have intoxicated a large part of German academic youth, is at least an evidence of the hunger for intellectual nourishment pent up in its rank and file. In no other country could such a book have produced such an effect. And the whole German *Jugendbewegung*, it may be added, is something entirely unique. That youth itself should philosophize about the idea of youth, should adopt the watchword, "Away from the sins of the fathers," should consciously rally for a new life of reveling in nature and in the great art of the past, and in moral matters should try to live up to the demand "in the midst of mean reality to profess a higher reality" — that could occur only in a country in which the striving for true cultivation of individual character, in contradistinction to a purely passive reception of external impressions, had been inherited from generation to generation and had become a part of the national character.

At least one consequence of this German cultivation of the inner life I wish to emphasize: the capacity to transform suffering into an impulse for higher activity. The whole history of modern Germany is one long story of national suffering, and at the same time a story of constant victories of countless anonymous individuals over the national suffering. What catastrophes have not swept over the German lands in the sixteenth, seventeenth, eighteenth, and nineteenth centuries. The sixteenth century brought, besides the terrible Peasants' War and the fearful massacres of Anabaptists, the clash between the Emperor and the Protestant princes in the Schmalkaldian War, and constant feuds between territorial princes and free cities; the seventeenth, not only the Thirty Years' War, but, after a short pause, new incursions by Swedes and French, the devastation of the Palatinate by Louis XIV, and the siege of Vienna by the Turks. The beginning of the eighteenth is filled with the wars of the Spanish and the Austrian Succession, largely waged upon German soil; its middle with the

GERMAN CHARACTER

Silesian campaigns and the Seven Years' War; its end and the beginning of the nineteenth with the inundation of all Germany by the armies of the French Revolution and Napoleon. Hardly a decade in these three centuries when wide provinces of the Empire were not ravaged and laid waste. And, in the midst of all this misery, a constant, ever-new gathering of vital forces, a slow, often interrupted, but never entirely repressed, ascent to spiritual greatness.

From this point of view, the very time of deepest political humiliation, the time from the Thirty Years' War to the accession of Frederick the Great, is seen to be a splendid manifestation of the constructive power of the spirit. For seldom has a people in the very breakdown of its political institutions so clearly proved its ability to rebuild its national culture. One generation after another, and one group of men by the side of another, devoted itself to this task. The brutalization of the masses and the fashionable degeneracy of the educated call forth, from the middle of the seventeenth century, in ever-widening circles of thinking men, patriotic indignation and attempts at the resurrection of national dignity in manners, speech, and feeling. The horrors of the war and the pressure of a servile subject-existence awaken the Stoic ideal of steadfastness and make calmness of soul a liberating power. The woes of the present make the tormented minds seek comfort in the study of ancient times and foreign countries, and thus help to create the science of universal history and ethnology.

And the work which Luther had begun, but had not been able to carry through — the foundation of religion upon the moral consciousness of the individual — is taken up once more in the midst of the national misery. Enlightened theologians, both of the Catholic and of the Protestant Church, pave the way for a reconciliation of fundamental creeds. Pietism opposes to dead ecclesiastical formulas the fervor of prayer and the duties of practical Christianity. Rationalism leads from the defects and imperfections of reality to the conception of a living universe, in which evil itself is made a power for good, and in which there seem to be evidences of a constant progress from lower to higher forms of life. And at last there emerges from these incessant and laborious efforts of respectable mediocrities the classic epoch of German genius.

We may indeed say that the best and noblest

possessions of the German people as a whole have been born from suffering; and perhaps we should be grateful to Fate that it has put the German people to trials in which it could prove itself great, not only in a few individual men, but also as a people. The last decade has been another such time of testing national worth. When has any nation, except Russia, in the short span of five years experienced so violent a convulsion, such an elemental upheaval of all its foundations of life, such mental distress, such a disintegration of whole classes of society, as the Germany thrown into the dust at Versailles? And to-day? Impoverished, humiliated, politically degraded, internationally gagged, is Germany even to-day. But this impoverished, humiliated, gagged nation possesses one thing which perhaps none of the victor nations possesses in the same degree: the belief in the spirit born from its sufferings, the burning desire for high achievements, the glowing wish to replace the loss of power by inner superiority, the firm determination to create a new national culture.

I have left to the end what is perhaps the most significant and most productive quality of German character in its best representatives — the wide intellectual horizon and the receptivity for the ideals of the universally human. I say deliberately "in its best representatives." For I do not wish to create the impression that I ignore such lamentable phenomena of mass psychosis as contemporary anti-Semitism or ultra-nationalist party fanaticism. These are phenomena which, lamentable as they are, find their explanation in particular social evils and particular political constellations. They do not belong to the great traditions of German culture. No other people has had a classic epoch of national culture which in cosmopolitanism, in breadth of horizon, and in detachment from inherited preconceptions could be compared with the age of classic German literature. From the æsthetic point of view this aloofness from the soil is an element of weakness in classic German literature; it gives to not a few of its creations something overrefined, too delicately spun, something shadowy, unreal. To realize this, one need only compare Goethe's *Iphigenie* with Shakespeare's *Julius Cæsar*, or Schiller's *Jungfrau von Orleans* with Bernard Shaw's *Saint Joan*. But in spiritual values, in pure humanity, in moral fervor and stimulus, the world of poetic imagination that sprung from the brains of Lessing, Goethe, and Schiller belongs to the very highest that has been achieved by any people of any age. Here we see, as hardly anywhere else, human personality in absolute freedom. Here the barriers of church, of race, of class, have been entirely eliminated. From *Nathan the Wise* to *Wallenstein*, *Wilhelm Tell*, and *Faust*, man is seen as such, in his eternal relations, his highest insights, his deepest conflicts, his mightiest strivings. A people which has accustomed itself to feel and live with such ideal figures as these is lifted thereby unconsciously to a higher level. And the fact that, in spite of many countercurrents, in spite of all critical attempts to belittle the grandeur of our classics, in spite of all the stars of lesser magnitude which have been glorified by Romanticism, Naturalism, Impressionism, and Expressionism, this ideal world of the German Classics has lost nothing of its lustre, but, on the contrary, throughout the nineteenth century and to this very day, in ever-increasing measure has come to be the spiritual treasure and support of the mass of the German people, is sufficient to prove the mission of Germany for the culture of the world.

IV

I close with a brief summing-up of the tasks which, as a result of all these reflections, seem to me the paramount duties of German-Americans, as heirs and guardians of German culture in this country. It seems to me clear that these tasks do not lie in the pursuit of group politics. We certainly should not abdicate our political rights. We should emphatically insist that the unworthy encroachments upon German equality, the neglects and injustices to American citizens of German descent, the abolition of German instruction in public schools, and similar outgrowths of war fanaticism, as far as they still exist, should speedily be revoked. We should do our best to win fuller understanding and sympathy with the present republican Germany in the American press, in the American institutions of learning, and among the American public in general. But the attempt to play a separate political rôle, to form a special German-American party, would not be what we owe to the country of our adoption. For, apart from the harmful results which such a racial policy would have for American party-life, it would not bring out what is best and most valua-

GERMAN CHARACTER

ble in German character; it would not represent the specifically German contribution to American civilization; it would not render to American life the specific service to which we, as German-Americans, are called. On the contrary, the formation of such a petty party-group, limited to the immediate interests of a particular set of people bound together by common descent, would be only a new and deplorable evidence of German lack of political farsightedness. That which is best and most valuable in German character, unless all my previous observations are mistaken, consists in independence of personality, in depth of conviction, in freedom from prejudice, in earnestness of intellectual effort, in breadth of view, in spiritual striving, in just appreciation of cultural values.

Let us cultivate, each in his own way, these precious legacies of our Old-World ancestry. Let us, like Carl Schurz, take our stand by the side of our fellow citizens of other descent as fully rounded personalities, bent on high achievements; let us take prominent part in all matters concerning the political, intellectual, moral, social, and artistic elevation of the masses; in other words, let us make use of the best of German culture in the service and for the benefit of our new fatherland. Through such a forward-looking attitude we shall win genuine respect for German character among our fellow citizens. And, above all, we shall in ever-increasing measure be in the front rank of those who are creating what is sacred to us all: the ideal America of the future.

IV

GERMAN AFTER-WAR IMAGINATION
(1926)

I

PESSIMISM is still the dominant note in the feelings that force themselves upon an observer of German conditions seven years after the pact of Versailles. To be sure, Germany has at last become a member of the League of Nations. And the recent conversations between M. Briand and Dr. Stresemann seem to justify the hope that the Locarno agreements will in not too distant a future at last be put into practice. For the moment, however, Germany still finds herself the only disarmed nation in the midst of neighbors armed as never before. And by far the larger part of the Rhineland is still occupied by allied troops, indeed suffers more from this occupation than before, since the troops withdrawn from the Cologne area have been simply transferred to the

Wiesbaden, Mainz, and Trier districts. Industrially, the country is in the grip of a deep depression. Tariff barriers, established by the very countries to which Germany owes reparations, and which might therefore be expected from sheer self-interest to foster the German export trade, have dealt this trade a heavy blow. Shipbuilding is practically at a standstill. One big industrial concern after another is facing bankruptcy. The unemployment figures of nearly two millions, added to the millions of middle-class people whose savings have been swept away by the inflation, make a terrible total of persons that must be fed from the public treasury or starve. In the city of Kiel, which, to be sure, has been particularly hard hit by the collapse in shipbuilding, at present nearly three-fifths of the population are dependent on public support. What this general state of enforced beggary means for the intellectual life may be illustrated by the fact that one of the foremost educational institutions of the world, the famous *Franckesche Stiftungen* at Halle, having lost its entire capital of ten million marks, finds it now impossible even to keep up its buildings in a state suitable for instruction. What makes this physical and intellectual suffering of

AFTER–WAR IMAGINATION

the German masses all the more galling is that to a very large extent Germany is still morally boycotted by the rest of the world. War hatred has been replaced by indifference: that is all. How many people are there in England, France, or the United States who seriously care whether Germany will succeed in the effort of reconstructing her national life on a democratic basis or not?

Gloomy and depressing as this situation is, the continued existence of Germany as a great and unified empire is no longer in doubt. For the very trials of the after-war period have disclosed an unexpectedly rich store of mental and moral power in the German people; they have revealed the fact that in spite of excruciating sufferings of four years of war and an equal number of years of perhaps still greater suffering after the war, there has remained in this people a surprisingly large reserve of what may be called practical imagination.

What has been achieved during the last few years by a determined will to find new ways of solving public difficulties and problems constitutes one of the most inspiring examples of what forces may be set in motion by freedom. For it is by relying on freedom that Germany is finding these new ways.

GERMAN AFTER-WAR PROBLEMS

American travellers returning from Europe are in the habit of extolling what Fascism is supposed to have accomplished in Italy, by promoting orderliness, thrift, industrial activity, and what not. They forget that all this show of national revival is based upon tyranny and militarism, that the Italian people is drunk with megalomania, that its glorification of war is a serious danger to international progress. How much more in accord with the best traditions of our country would these Americans be, if they took the trouble to visit Germany and to enlighten us about the strides which freedom is making there.

All the most important steps recently taken by the German Government — particularly the stabilization of the currency and the guaranty proposals for permanent peace — were appeals to the practical imagination, involving great individual sacrifices, but also offering great possibilities for the common welfare; and all have been met with popular approval of the most unmistakable sort. The result has been that, with the exception of the academic and aristocratic diehards, particularly of Bavaria and Prussia, whose power of making noise, by the way, seems to be in inverse ratio to their inner strength, monarchism

AFTER-WAR IMAGINATION

with its attendant appeal to military glory is rapidly disappearing; that the Republic, to the vast majority of the German people, has come to be the symbol of reconstruction and progress; and that participation in this work of reconstruction gives to the mass of the people a firm and ardent faith in Germany's future.

How automatically, one might say, the whole trend of German political imagination is toward strengthening the foundations of free institutions, is strikingly shown by the careers of the first two Presidents of the Republic: Ebert and Hindenburg. Ebert, although elected to the Presidency as the leader of the then most powerful party — the Socialist — ceased to be a party leader from the moment he became President. Throughout his nearly seven years of office he persistently stood above parties and did his best in every crisis to bring about a compromise between the conflicting factions. And Hindenburg, from whose accession a monarchist reaction was either hoped or feared, has most happily disappointed both the supporters and the opponents of his candidacy. Although royalist by long tradition and service, he has withstood all temptations to be drawn into royalist intrigues; although in every fibre a soldier, he has steadfastly supported the policy that led to Locarno; although a natural commander, he has spurned every ambition of dictatorship. No man could be a fitter guardian of the freedom won for Germany by disaster and ruin.

So it has come to pass that the political machinery set up only seven years ago by the Weimar National Assembly is running with a smoothness as if Germany has been used to republican government for generations. Parliamentary deadlocks resulting from the multiplicity of parties bitterly opposed to each other do not in the long run block the progress of legislation. Ministerial crises are habitually, if not very fundamentally, adjusted. Elections and referendums call out voters in numbers of percentage usually surpassing those in the United States, and pass off with remarkable quiet and orderliness. Of particular significance was the referendum held last June concerning the proposed sequestration of the estates of all the former royal and princely dynasties. A heated campaign had preceded it, but the voting day itself led to no serious disturbances anywhere; and the result — the vetoing of the proposal — was accepted with the same equanim-

AFTER-WAR IMAGINATION

ity and submission to the people's voice which has so often been praised — and rightly so — as a manifestation of true democracy in American Presidential elections. The calm acceptance of defeat in this particular case, to be sure, rested undoubtedly in part on the fact that, after all, the vote had shown so large a number of people in favor of the measure (nearly 15 million out of a total of 30 million possible voters), that it surely would have become law had not the opponents largely refrained from voting, so as to keep the whole vote cast under 20 million, the legal minimum for the adoption of any referendum proposal. The outcome, then, of last June's referendum has in every way been fortunate. It has proved, on the one hand, that Germany is overwhelmingly republican; and it has, on the other hand, prevented sequestration of royal property without compensation, and has left the disposition of this property to the only proper method — that of a compromise between the former rulers and the present governments of the individual states. Republican Germany is not going to be bolshevist.

In the midst of privations, then, such as the average American has no conception of, in the midst of widespread physical suffering, the Germany of to-day has regained her mental equilibrium. She is again making a place for herself in the political and industrial field; she is trying to use the mass of unemployed for public improvements of every sort; she is maintaining, though at the greatest sacrifices, her workingmen's insurance laws, established in the decades before the war; she is reviving her merchant marine; she is making good for her loss of coal in Silesia and the Saar by an extraordinary enlargement of her lignite production; she is reorganizing her school system on a democratic basis; she is returning in a large measure to the oldtime orderliness, cleanliness, and modest joyfulness of the daily life of the common man. All these achievements may be called the result of practical imagination, stimulated by distress and bitter necessity.

II

Is a similar revival observable in matters pertaining to the literary and artistic imagination? I am free to confess that I am somewhat puzzled how to answer this question.

One thing seems to be clear. The present state of the imaginative arts in Germany is not an isolated phenomenon, it is a part of the emotional convulsion into which the whole world has been plunged by the Great War. The life of all the civilized nations since the last decades of the nineteenth century had in a constantly increasing measure been absorbed by materialism, by reckless competition, and national greed. The war, in spite of the fine illusions of the millions who were sacrificed to it, was only the mad climax of the universal craving for brute power and primitive self assertion. No wonder that the extent to which it aroused and intensified the savage instincts among all nations is perhaps without parallel in history.

This world-wide brutalization of life has left its trace, or rather has come to the surface, even more hideously after the war than during it. Wherever we turn, we see the same loosening of moral restraint, the same hysteria and excitability, the same acceptance of aggressive nudity in women, the same connivance with uncontrolled appetites in men. And the productions of the literary and artistic imagination reflecting this international condition of things are consequently in all countries prevailingly disquieting, unsettling, and questionable. But I doubt whether this state of inner disintegration and subversion of normal life is anywhere as strikingly manifested as in most recent German literature and art.

Far be it from me to underestimate the significance of what these German dramas, novels, lyric poems, paintings, or sculptures of the last few years have to offer to the historical student if looked upon as eruptions of social diseases, as echoes of human suffering and misery, as calls for revolt, or as symbols of the ideals of a world not yet born. Mr. Herman George Scheffauer, in his recent book, "The New Vision in German Arts,"[1] has presented, with a good deal of force and persuasiveness, this aspect of what we have become accustomed to call Expressionism. Who would not be deeply stirred by such a drama as Ernst Toller's "Masse Mensch" (*Man in the Mass*), with its wild phantasmagoria of all the evil forces of modern civilization — the brute power of the state, the brute power of capital, the brute power of the ignorant, degraded masses — moving together in terrible unison, like parts of a monstrous gigantic machinery, relentlessly grinding down the poor human soul caught in its

[1] Published by the Viking Press, New York.

wheels. Who would not feel reverberating in himself the utter reversal of all accepted standards of conduct brought about by the Great War in the extraordinary happenings of such a novel as Jakob Wassermann's [1] "Faber or the Lost Years" — the aberrations, delusions, phantastic aspirations of people, cut loose from their moorings, estranged to themselves, drifting about in a sea of morbid sensations and whimsical attempts to regain control over a life which they no longer understand. Who could remain indifferent to the world of nameless longing, inarticulate mysticism, mute despair, black contrition, stammering joy, dimly phantastic visions, and sudden, dazzling inner illuminations revealed in such a book of verse as Franz Werfel's "Der Gerichtstag" (*Doomsday*). And who would deny that the very crudities, distortions, and hallucinations of expressionistic painting and sculpture — such as Otto Dix's "War," or Franz Marc's "Tower of Blue Horses," [2] or Kandinsky's kaleidoscopic

[1] That Wassermann's literary manner is deliberately impressionist rather than impulsively expressionist, is obvious.

[2] Although not an after-war production (Marc was killed in the war), this painting, now in the Berlin National Gallery, acquired its standing in public estimation as a classic of German expressionism in the years after the war.

riddles or Wauer's "Man's Impotent Reaching into the Universe"—are at least attempts, however unintelligible or repulsive, to create a world of images totally different from that which spreads itself before the eyes of the majority of men, the uninitiated and unsophisticated.

If, however, we approach these and similar productions not as historical phenomena but simply as works of art, our judgment will naturally take a different turn. A personal experience that came to me in Europe a few months ago may perhaps illustrate what I mean.

Stopping for a short time in Florence on my way to Germany, I devoted one morning to revisiting both San Marco and San Lorenzo. Nearly simultaneously, then, there were crowded upon me renewed impressions of two supreme masterpieces of art which in subject, execution, and temper form the greatest possible contrast to each other: Fra Angelico's ascetic figures of the great Saints of the mediæval Church assembled before the Crucifixion group, and Michelangelo's four gigantic embodiments of time reclining in front of the Medici tombs. On the one hand, the triumph of the spirit over the flesh, monastic self-denial, chaste retirement, mystic contemplation, rapturous devotion, childlike trust, heavenly transfiguration; on the other, glorification of the naked body, revelling in sinewy strength and heroic manhood, fearless revealing of woman's beauty, apotheosis of the will, the life of the senses at its height. And yet, the effect upon me of these two impressions so radically different was essentially the same. Never before, it seemed to me, had I felt the affinity of genius so clearly. I felt certain that only by mastering themselves, by concentrating all their powers, by conquering everything low and mean within themselves, could these two masters have risen to such creations. And I also felt that only by trying in my humble way to hold myself together, to overcome my weaknesses and failures, to be my real self, could I rise to even a faint realization of the greatness of these two supreme masterpieces. The incentive, then, to such a widening, heightening, and intensifying of my own personality seemed to me the true and essential effect of those great works of art upon my imagination.

When later in Switzerland, on Lake Thun, I plunged into reading contemporary German literature, hoping to get a vivifying breath of the new life that I knew was springing up in the land of my birth, I had an experience directly opposite to that in San Marco and San Lorenzo. I seemed to see before me a great array of youthful talent, an impulsive striving for new forms, a high sensitiveness to the fundamental problems of life, a burning desire to say the ultimate things and to unlock the riddles of the universe. But instead of the self-discipline and self-mastery needed for such a task, I found ecstatic ravings and hysterical exaggerations, not to speak of the unabashed sensual libido which often formed the sorry counterpart to all this sublimated and hyper-refined emotionalism. Instead of being strengthened and raised to my own better self, I felt weakened and degraded by much of this reading, and often I could not prevail upon myself to open these books in the face of the wonderful Alpine world that looked down in its unstained grandeur upon my garden.

A similar feeling came over me when later in the summer I visited art galleries and art expositions in Germany and there had an opportunity to compare the work of Menzel, Lenbach, Leibl, Liebermann, and other representatives of the best in German art of the nineteenth century with the irresponsible daubings and hideous lunacies of the mass of Expressionists who from the wreck of the old order of things seem to have rescued nothing but the cult of their own pretentious and erratic selves. And most regretfully I came to the conclusion that the mass of German literary and artistic output of to-day is, after all, prevailingly a symptom of disintegration, that it stands for recklessness rather than liberty, that its effect particularly upon the growing generation must be disconcerting rather than upbuilding, that, in a word, it is a confirmation of Goethe's solemn warning:

> *Vergebens werden ungebundene Geister*
> *Nach der Vollendung reiner Höhe streben.*
> *Wer Grosses will muss sich zusammen raffen.*
> *In der Beschränkung zeigt sich erst der Meister*
> *Und das Gesetz nur kann uns Freiheit geben.*

III

And yet, there are signs that the new freedom which in spite of temporary defeats and failures is gradually restoring Germany to her social and political equilibrium, is in æsthetic matters also bringing back something of that restraint and self-mastery which are the necessary prerequisites for truly great creations.

GERMAN AFTER-WAR PROBLEMS

Two writers of very different make-up stand out, to my mind, as conspicuously striking instances of this encouraging tendency: Franz Werfel and Thomas Mann.

Werfel, now in the middle thirties, was known before the war as a writer of youthful lyric effusions of strange elusiveness and sibyllinic profundity. The war — in which, by the way, he served with the Austrian army at the Galician and Serbian fronts — seems to have aroused in him nothing but horror and loathing. But it cannot have helped tinging his fervid feeling for humanity with an even deeper and more ardent hue than it had before. In a number of dramas, partly symbolic, partly of extreme naturalism, which after the restoration of peace followed each other in quick succession, he displayed an ever-increasing power of presenting the heights as well as the depths of life, most brilliantly perhaps in an extraordinary spiritual extravaganza — "Spiegelmensch" (*Mirror-man*) — in which the God-Satan of the human breast appears and reappears in a truly dazzling multitude of fugitive and constantly shifting shapes. But the work in which Werfel first attained structural mastery combined with genuine grasp of human character is, I think, his novel "Verdi," a truly noble monument to the great composer's memory.[1]

Verdi is seen here as an old man, in his seventieth year; but in retrospect, through his own eyes, his whole previous life, so rich in achievements, afflictions, and triumphs, passes before us in review. For the last decade, he has suffered from an invincible apathy of spirit. He hardly dares to confess to himself that the source of his depression is to be found in the name Richard Wagner. For he is too noble, too generous a nature to be susceptible to anything resembling envy. But yet, it is so. Wagner's fame, Wagner's domineering and monopolizing personality, the spell which his gigantic productions exercise over the whole of Europe, have paralyzed Verdi's productivity; since his last phenomenal success, the "Aida," he has achieved nothing. In vain has he labored year after year over a libretto of "King Lear," in which he has been trying to give vent to all this gloom and despair. Now he is determined upon a last attempt, he has retired incognito to a hotel in Venice, in the seclusion of which he hopes to finish the score.

[1] Published in 1923; an English translation (Simon & Schuster, New York) appeared in 1925.

GERMAN AFTER-WAR PROBLEMS

It is the same year, 1883, in which Wagner, a few months before his death, was accorded his last popular triumph, the reception and glorification by the Venetian aristocracy. Verdi knows, of course, of his rival's presence in the city. Indeed, he has come partly on that account. He wants to see him, to meet him, to confront him. He even witnesses, uninvited and unobserved, one of the social functions in his honor. But he cannot prevail upon himself to make himself known. He avoids the opportunity which he had sought. He buries himself in his work, wrestling alone with his thought and his fancies. The great moments of his life — catastrophes, trials, victories — pass before him in these lonely hours: the poverty of his boyhood, the early years of laborious and modest conductorship, the death of his young wife and his two little children, the utter stupefaction following it, the crushing fiasco of an attempt in comic opera, the astounding success of the great operas of his middle manhood, and then — the stagnation, the unaccountable stagnation. Why should it be? How could it be? Does he not feel himself musically superior to this Wagner? Does he not know that his melody is born from instinct, from natural oneness with the genius of his race, not, like Wagner's huge constructions, from conscious artifice? And this "Lear," will it not show the world that he too has learned something from the German's technique? that he is still young? that he is still master of the whole scale of human emotions? So he struggles on, ardently, feverishly, but hopeless, never sure of himself, never really trusting his own genius. On Carnival night, he sees Wagner for a second time, in the midst of the multitude swaying to and fro on the Piazza di San Marco, where a band is playing miscellaneous pieces. A potpourri from "Aida" has just begun. Breathlessly Verdi watches his "enemy" from the distance to see what impression the music makes upon him. But Wagner, eagerly talking, as always, to his companions, pays little attention to the selection, and finally, after listening for a few minutes, even seems to make a wearied and dissatisfied gesture. Again Verdi feels petrified, again the impulse to speak to the great man is checked. He drifts away with the crowd. Late in the evening he finds himself in front of the huge pyre on which the climax of the fête, the burning of King Carnival, is enacted. Disturbed, excited by the weird, intoxicating scenes of the fantastic night, he returns to his room. Exhausted he sinks into his chair by the fireplace. Again the tragedy of his life, the futility of his efforts, the impossibility of regaining his youthful productivity rise before him in ghastly, exaggerated forms. He cannot resist the spectres. With both hands he seizes the score of "King Lear" and hurls the whole manuscript, the work of a decade, into the flames.

The composite effect of this deed of madness is a spiritual upheaval. First it is a kind of relief at a sacrificial act having been done. Then follows stupor at the realization of the irreparable loss. Then a bodily swoon in which he sees himself face to face with death. When he awakes from the swoon, the oppression of years, the laming sense of inferiority, all degrading jealousy are gone. He feels happy, he sees life clearly, he feels the brotherhood of all human fate, he is sure that he has misjudged Wagner, that they will understand each other, he decides to go to the Palazzo Vendramin and call upon him. When he arrives at the palace, he hears that Wagner has just died.

And thus are ushered in the nearly twenty years of Verdi's high old age, serene, magnanimous, fertile, crowned by two of his greatest masterpieces: "Otello" and "Falstaff."

AFTER-WAR IMAGINATION

I need not say that this bare summary of the principal inner conflict of the novel gives no idea whatever of the richness of life in which it abounds. It fairly overflows with romantic — perhaps too romantic — adventures, with striking characters, with bold — perhaps too bold — situations, with the whole fascinating, bewildering beauty and voluptuousness which the name Venice implies. But at least I hope to have made it apparent that Werfel was fully justified when he appropriated for his own benefit a word of the old Maestro himself: "To reproduce truth may be good, but to invent truth is better, far better."

That, as a dramatist also, Werfel is reaching out for a new style, for a combination of romantic fullness of life with classic succinctness of form, is clearly seen in the tragedy which at present is making the round of the German theatres: "Juarez und Maximilian." As I happened unfortunately to be prevented from seeing it performed last summer, I cannot judge of its stage effect, although I should think that it would carry its audience swiftly from scene to scene.[1] But about the human quality of this representation of

---

[1] Its recent production by the Theatre Guild of New York seems to have been a somewhat doubtful success.

the Mexican adventure of Napoleon III and the Hapsburgs there can be no doubt. Although Juarez does not appear on the stage at all, the compelling influence of his master mind, his cool fierceness, and his inexorable logic is ever present throughout the play, forming a striking contrast to the impulsiveness, chivalry, and sentimentalism of the ill-starred Emperor. A great variety of minor characters, lightly but tellingly sketched, give lively color to the action: the gross, plebeian, unreliable Bazaine, the intriguing and unscrupulous Archbishop Labatista, the traitorous courtier Lopez, the gallant and high-minded Porfirio Diaz, the noble and impassioned Empress, the loyally devoted Austrian entourage of the imperial household. Maximilian himself, in spite of his weaknesses and inconsistencies — or perhaps because of them — has touches of true human pathos. His is the tragedy of the man of good will who is forced to do wrong, of the humanitarian who becomes an oppressor, of the idealist who is led into atrocities. He has accepted the Mexican crown, believing himself destined to perform a sacred mission: the mission of atoning for the wrong done to Mexico by the Spanish conquest. He dreams of bringing peace, happiness, education, social progress to the mass of the oppressed and ignorant natives. Instead, he finds himself the tool of political schemers, financial speculators, clerical reactionaries, cruel upholders of class monopoly. He is deceived into the attempt to save his tottering throne by signing a decree of reckless massacre. He is terrified by the slaughter resulting from it, he longs to suffer for his guilt. Death comes to be to him not so much an atonement as a necessity, an expression of his own inner, better, purer self. "I want to *live* my death," is his word of farewell before facing his executioners.

Brilliant and well-nigh inexhaustible in its truly Austrian buoyancy of temper as Werfel's imagination is, it cannot be compared in depth and power with that of the North-German Thomas Mann. Indeed, among all contemporary German writers of fiction, Thomas Mann stands out as a solitary and unique figure. From the year 1901, the date of his first great novel, *Die Buddenbrooks*, until the beginning of the war, keeping conspicuously aloof from the sentimental emotionalism of the Herzogs and Frenssens, steadfastly maintaining his careful, serious, austere manner of observation, his profound insight into character, his sure grasp of the things of the outer world, he allowed to be published only such productions of his as came fully up to the standard of his own judicious and severe self-scrutiny. During the war, he refused to be drawn into any kind of hysteria, seeking solace in retirement and in deep studies upon the basic qualities of German national achievements and failures. But not until a year ago, seven years after the armistice, as a man of fifty, has he given us, as the finished product of a whole decade of work, thought, investigation, suffering, and striving, what perhaps will go down in history as the most subtle spiritual reflex of an age of convulsions, disruptions, and cataclysms — the two-volume novel *Der Zauberberg*.

I shall not attempt the impossible by trying to give an account of the extraordinary variety of characters and happenings which Thomas Mann crowds together on the stage of this "Mount of Enchantment," a luxurious international tuberculosis sanatorium in the midst of the snow and icefields of Davos. The author himself, in an answer to critics, has admitted that it was meant by him as representative of the diseased capitalistic society of pre-war Europe, the very society upon which rests the ultimate guilt of having made the

AFTER-WAR IMAGINATION

war inevitable. But this social symbolism of the underlying conception reveals itself only now and then to the more deeply searching eye, and then only dimly; it does not in the least take away from the vividness and reality of the individual experiences brought before us. What most palpably is the common theme of all these individual experiences is Death — death and its relation to life.

At first sight it is the grimly farcical aspect of death that forces itself upon us as the prevailing impression of this picture. The society congregated on lonely Alpine heights in its flight from the fatal result of disease, contracted in the conflux and tumult of modern civilization, seems habitually to be engaged in a veritable *Danse Macabre*. Although bearing the mark of Death upon their faces, the majority of them keep on following the course of their mean and worthless habits. Indeed, the disease only accentuates their weaknesses and their appetites; it makes them caricatures of life; and all their eating, drinking, flirting, gossiping, bragging, slandering, and intriguing is nothing but one continuous, though constantly changing, collective grimace. A few figures, however, stand out by contrast from this mass of frivolity and vulgarity.

GERMAN AFTER-WAR PROBLEMS

There is the young German officer, Joachim Ziemssen, instinctively guarding himself against the weakening influences of his illness and the equivocal charms of his effete surroundings, holding himself inwardly and outwardly erect, bent only upon regaining his health and rejoining the colors: his final succumbing to the fatal disease has a fine human touch and affects us like a soldier's death on the battlefield. There is the ascetic Italian humanist and philosopher, Signor Settembrini, a champion of the spirit, an enthusiastic advocate of freedom, enlightenment, and progress, a living protest against self-indulgence and weakness of the flesh: his brilliant speeches on human dignity and the necessity of resisting bodily conditions dispel for the moment the enervating air of the sick-room. There is Settembrini's spiritual antagonist, the Galician ex-Jew and revolutionary Jesuit Naphta, a fanatic of skepticism, nihilism, terrorism, despotism: his provoking and defiant attacks against phrases and fashions and the whole existing order of things stimulate intellectual independence and courage, although they lead to his own rash and unhappy end. There is the aged Dutch tobacco-king, Mynheer Peeperkorn, a giant of living, of enjoyment, of feeling, truly Gargantuesque in his proportions: his primitive massiveness and impressiveness seem to contradict all impotence and inactivity, and his suicide impresses us like the blasting of rocks. And there is the principal figure of the novel, the young Hamburg patrician Hans Castorp, in whom all the fantastic sights and experiences of this world of fever, decay, and death produce a complete reversal of his former commonplace states of mind and views of life.

He is an ingenuous youth of aristocratic and refined instincts, not in any way remarkable intellectually, dreamy and indolent, highly impressionable. He joins the sanatorium company in the first place on a brief vacation trip as the guest of his cousin, Joachim Ziemssen, is therefore in the first place only a sympathetic observer of the effects of disease upon different natures and tempers. But soon he finds himself a patient too, and gradually drifts into a state where disease as such comes to be his all-absorbing study and occupation. Of striking outward experiences there is very little. The weeks, seasons, years come and go. Time seems to lose all distinguishing features. An immeasurable sameness of arrival and departure, of X-ray examinations and lung operations, of dying and recovering, of frivolous amusement and of lonely despair, of superlatively blue sky and savagely violent snowstorms envelops all things. The silence of eternity seems to descend. But in this silent sameness of things Hans Castorp hears voices and sees sights which stir his innermost being.

Soon after his arrival he has noticed in the dining room, at the "Russian table," far from his own, a young woman whose face, manner, motions strangely attract him. He learns that she is the wife of a Russian official beyond the Caucasus whom, however, no one has ever seen here, that she is tubercular, that she is a frequenter of all the fashionable European health resorts — Madame Chauchat. For months and months he makes no attempt to be introduced to her, nor does she speak to him when they accidentally meet in the halls or the parkways. But her seductive image pursues him always and everywhere; at meal times his glance is constantly trying to meet hers, sometimes successfully; in his room he examines his temperature and is delighted to find that his fever rises at the thought of her; he dreams of her kiss at night. He knows that all this is immoral, that it is disease. But is not disease a heightened condition of life? Does it not open your eyes to the mystery of things? Does it not give you a freedom of which the workaday world has no conception? And are not love and disease the same thing? Do they not both disintegrate the body? Do they not both lead to death — death, the glorifier of all things, the solemn and majestic power which transforms life and surrounds it with eternity? By such and similar sophistries does this modern Tristan try to justify to himself his inner looseness and to assimilate the poison from which he cannot escape.

That this hysterical state of mind does indeed expand and heighten his soul life is apparent. It makes him peculiarly susceptible to the suffering round about him and induces him to shower all kinds of attention and kindnesses upon particularly distressing cases among his fellow patients, the incurable, the moribund, the utterly lonely. It makes him listen with feverish eagerness to the debates of his philosophic friends about human freedom and destiny. It makes him delve in an amateurish way into the abstruse recesses of modern biology and chemistry. But everywhere he finds a confirmation of the conviction which more and more firmly and inevitably is settling upon him — the conviction that his whole previous life of health and activity had been a delusion, that only on this Mount of Enchantment has he come to understand the source of all our highest feelings and deepest insights: death.

So he drifts on, dreaming and longing. Only twice in the book is there a meeting of the lovers, if lovers they can be called. The first time at a fancy-dress party on Carnival Tuesday, the evening before Madame Chauchat's departure. Here Hans Castorp, emboldened by the Bohemian license of the fête, approaches her without ceremony, addresses her with "Du," blurts out before her his fantastic philosophy, and trembling, on his knees, stammers insane words about the wondrous mystery of her body and the raptures of eternal communion; while she, stroking his hair, half tempting, half pitying, calls him "petit bourgeois" and "mon prince Carnaval."

The second meeting, years later, is after her return with another "travelling companion," the Gargantuesque Mynheer Peeperkorn. This time it is she who makes the first approach. On the basis of their common feelings for the marvellous old man who has impressed his personality upon both of them, she asks and receives Hans Castorp's consent to a treaty of friendship; and she seals this treaty with a kiss. But although these are the only two scenes in which the Russian adventuress and the young German ingénu engage in intimate conversation, we feel her spell throughout the book and are made to understand why with her final departure all incentive seems to have gone from him.

He now sinks back into what the author calls "the great dullness"— the ordinary dallying away of time by the sanatorium company, stamp-collecting, amateur photography, esperanto, playing patience, and what not; he becomes a victrola fanatic, a victim of hypnotism and spiritistic séances; he even takes an interest in all the silly and stupid altercations and enmities which infest the hospital atmosphere. He seems to have lost his individuality.

What at last arouses and restores him to himself is the great historic thunderclap which rocks the foundations of the Mount of Enchantment and scatters its inhabitants to the four winds: the declaration of war.

"The dreamer stood up and looked about himself. He felt disenchanted, redeemed, delivered — not through his own will power, as he had to confess to himself with a sense of shame, but hurled into space by elemental forces to which his deliverance was an entirely accidental and secondary matter. But although his little fate vanished into nothing before the universal disaster, was here not after all a revelation of something like personal, that is, divine justice and grace? If life was to accept once more her sinful child of sorrows — not on easy terms, but in the hard and harsh manner of a visitation which perhaps did not mean bodily life, but three volleys of honor over his, the sinner's, grave, then he was ready for it. And thus he sank down on his knees, face and hands lifted up to a sky which was sulphurous and dark, but not any longer the grotto ceiling of the Mount of Sin."

The final scene shows him on the battlefield, as a private, mudbespattered, gun in hand, in the midst of falling comrades, blindly plunging on into shot and shell.

I know that I have given only a very imperfect impression of a book crowded — possibly overcrowded — with thought, with knowledge, with characters, with incidents. But perhaps I have made it clear that it is essentially an epic of the inner life, and that, morbid and irrational as is its subject, it appeals altogether to the striving for health and reason. In reading it, I could not help recalling the sensations aroused in me by the masterpieces of San Marco and San Lorenzo; for here also I felt the power of an artist who, concentrating his whole being upon his work, disciplining his will and his imagination, presenting life with perfect detachment and sovereignty of mind, has by this mastery of himself created something which communicates to those who enter into his work the same firm and self-controlled state of feeling. And, as a German, I could not help being proud that a work of such calm greatness and fundamental nobility should have sprung from the soil of harassed and distracted Germany.

IV

Only a blind optimism would minimize the grave and threatening dangers which still beset the future of Europe. Will the German people be able to bear indefinitely the ever-increasing burden of reparations? Will the racial antipathies and resentments, kept alive by the occupation of the Rhineland as well as by the conditions prevailing in the Polish Corridor, be ultimately allayed through some sort of compromise? Will the rights of national minorities be more effectively guarded by the League of Nations than heretofore? Will the disarmament plans lead to tangible results? None of these questions can be answered in the affirmative with any degree of assurance.

That, in the midst of all these perplexing problems, Germany should have set her face resolutely toward peace, that, avoiding dictatorship on the one hand and anarchy on the other, she should have made long strides in organizing freedom, is one of the few unreservedly hopeful symptoms of the times.

If, by the development of her inner resources, by the cultivation of her intellectual and moral heritage, by demonstrating her right to international leadership in the realm of the spirit, she succeeds in replacing what she has lost in outward power, she will be the foremost safeguard of European tranquillity, happiness, and enlightenment in the decades to come.

INDEX

INDEX

Absolutism, Era of, 72.
America, United States of, 31, 53 ff.
Angelico, Fra, 106 f.
Augsburg, Romantic Week in, 12.

Bach, J. B., 78.
Bebel, Aug., 75.
Beethoven's *Missa Solemnis*, 15.
Bismarck, 4, 19 f., 74 f., 81.
Briand, A., 95.
Buddhism, 39 ff.
Byron's *Manfred*, 16.

Calvin, 63.
China, 50 ff.
Christianity, 39, 42, 63.
Confucianism, 50 f.
Cosmopolitanism of Classic German literature, 90 f.

Damaschke, A. W. F., 13.
Darmstadt, "School of Wisdom" in, 26, 37.
Dix, Otto, 105.

Ebert, President, 99.
Einstein, A., 15.
England, 30.
Euckenbund, 13.
Expressionism, 104 ff., 109.

Fichte, 80 f.
Foerster, F. W., 18 ff., 34.
Franckesche Stiftungen at Halle, 96.

INDEX

German-Americans, 68, 92 f.
German bourgeoisie, 75 f.
German character, 28 f., 68–91.
German Empire, The Mediæval, 69 f.
German industrials, 31 ff.
Goethe, 15 f., 80, 90.

Händel festivals at Göttingen, 13.
Hauptmann's *Weavers*, 15.
Hebbel, Fr., 81.
Hindenburg, 99 f.
Hinduism, 39 ff., 53.
Hofmannsthal's *Everyman*, 17.
Holbein's *Dance of Death*, 17.

Italy, 98.

Japan, 57 f.

Kandinsky, W., 105.
Kant, 42, 47 f., 51, 79.
Keyserling, H., 18, 25 ff., 35–67, 68.
Kieler Herbstwoche, 14 ff.
Kleist, H. von, 81.
Klopstock, 78.
Kulturkampf, 75.

Lessing, 78 f., 90 f.
Liberation, Wars of, 73.
Liebknecht, W., 75.
Luther, 63, 71, 77 f., 88.

Mann, Heinrich, 77.
Mann, Thomas, 68, 77, 110, 117–127.
Marc, Franz, 105.
Michelangelo, 106 f.
Monarchism, 98 f.

INDEX

Nietzsche, 3, 28, 77, 82.

Perfection, Hindu ideal of, 42 ff., 59.
Pietism, 88.
Progress, American absorption in, 59 f.
Prussia, 19, 72.

Rationalism, 88.
Referendum, 100 f.
Reformation, The, 70 f.
Reger, Max, 17.
Republicanism, 99 f.
Restoration, Era of the, 73 f.
Revolution of 1848, 74.
Russell, Bertrand, 56.

Scheffauer, H. G., 104.
Schiller, 79 f., 90.
Schurz, 82, 93.
Shakespeare, 17, 90.
Shaw, G. B., 90.
Socialism, 29 f.
Spengler, Oswald, 6 ff., 84 f.
State, Conception of, 23 f.
Steiner, R., 18, 22 ff., 34.
Stresemann, G., 95.
Strindberg's *Spectre-Sonata*, 17.
Suffering, Effect of, upon German character, 86 ff.

Tagore, Rabindranath, 49.
Thirty Years' War, Recovery from, 87 f.
Toller, Ernst, 104.

Wagner, R., 16, 81, 111 ff.
Wassermann, Jakob, 105.
Wauer, W., 106.

INDEX

Weimar Constitution, 6, 100.
Werfel, Franz, 105, 110–117.
Wilhelminian Era, 4 f., 23 f., 28, 31, 75 f.
World-consciousness, The new, 66 f.

Yoga, 44 f.
Youth Movement, The German, 12 f., 85 f.